STUDY GUIDE

CHRISTINE STAMM
LINDA CULLEN

ON COOKING

A TEXTBOOK OF CULINARY FUNDAMENTALS

SECOND EDITION

SARAH R. LABENSKY
ALAN M. HAUSE

DRAWINGS BY STACEY WINTERS QUATTRONE

PRENTICE HALL

UPPER SADDLE RIVER, NEW JERSEY 07458

Acquisitions editor: NEIL MARQUARDT
Editorial assistant: JEAN AUMAN
Development editor: JUDITH CASILLO
Marketing manager: FRANK MORTIMER, JR.
Cover design: RUTA K. FIORINO
Cover photograph: STOCKFOOD/EISING
Copyeditor: NANCY VELTHAUS
Manufacturing manager: ED O'DOUGHERTY
Director of production and manufacturing: BRUCE JOHNSON
Managing editor: MARY CARNIS
Production editor: LARRY HAYDEN IV

Printed in the United States of America
10 9 8 7 6 5 4 3 2 1

ISBN 0-13-973256-X

Prentice-Hall International (UK) Limited, *London*
Prentice-Hall of Australia Pty. Limited, *Sydney*
Prentice-Hall Canada Inc., *Toronto*
Prentice-Hall Hispanoamericana, S.A., *Mexico City*
Prentice-Hall of India Private Limited, *New Delhi*
Prentice-Hall of Japan, Inc., *Tokyo*
Simon & Schuster Asia Pte. Ltd., *Singapore*
Editora Prentice-Hall do Brasil, Ltda., *Rio de Janeiro*

CONTENTS

About the Authors

Chef Christine Stamm is an experienced culinarian and an Associate Professor at Johnson & Wales University's College of Culinary Arts in Providence, Rhode Island where she has taught for the past nine years. She teaches a variety of laboratory courses in the Associate of Applied Science and Bachelor of Science degree programs in Culinary Arts.

Christine has earned an A.O.S. degree in Culinary Arts, a Bachelor of Science degree in Foodservice Management, a Masters degree in Management Technology, and currently maintains A.B.D. status in pursuit of her Doctorate degree in Education at Boston University. In addition, she is certified by the American Culinary Federation as a Working Chef. She has achieved national acclaim, winning several local and international gold awards in food show competitions such as Hotelympia in London, England; Chef Ireland; and the Culinary Olympics in Frankfurt, Germany. Outside of teaching, she serves as a foodservice consultant and lecturer.

Linda Cullen is an experienced culinarian, having held positions as chef manager and head chef in various establishments. Linda holds a Bachelor of Science degree in foodservice management and a Master of Science degree in managerial technology. For the past two years, Linda has been active in the Newport chapter of the American Culinary Federation, where she was editor of the chapter communique and is currently secretary.

In addition, Linda is a certified Culinary Educator. She has won awards for her culinary skill, including winning a gold medal at the prestigious International Culinary Exhibition at Torquay in England.

PROFESSIONALISM

TEST YOUR KNOWLEDGE

The practice sets provided below have been designed to test your comprehension of the information found in this chapter. It is recommended that you read this chapter completely before attempting these questions.

1A. Terminology

Fill in the blank spaces with the correct definition.

   1. Brigade   _____

   2. Gourmand   _____

   3. Nouvelle cuisine   _____

   4. Sous chef   _____

   5. Grande cuisine   _____

   6. Fernand Point   _____

   7. Classic cuisine   _____

   8. Executive chef   _____

   9. Dining room manager   _____

10. Marie-Anton Carême   _____

11. Line cooks   _____

12. Auguste Escoffier   _____

13. Pastry chef _____

14. Area chef _____

15. Head waiter _____

1B. Fill in the Blank

Fill in the blanks provided with the response that correctly completes the statement.

1. _____ is terminology used in reference to the foodservice industry to describe the area where guests are generally not allowed, such as the kitchen.

2. _____ service tends to be more formal by using two waiters: a captain and a waiter.

3. _____ is terminology used in reference to the foodservice industry to describe the area where guests are welcome and serviced, such as the dining room.

4. In _____ service, the entree, vegetables, and potatoes are served from a platter onto a plate by the waiter.

5. A_____ _____ is responsible for making sure the tables are properly set, foods are delivered in a timely fashion to the proper tables, and that the guests' needs are met.

6. In _____ service, one waiter takes the order and brings the food to the table.

7. _____ is another term used for the position of the dining room attendant, who clears plates and refills water glasses at various tables in the dining room.

1C. Short Answer

Provide a short response that correctly answers each of the questions below.

1. List three (3) advantages that the introduction of the cast iron stove lent to professional, 19th century cooking.

   a. _____

   b. _____

   c. _____

2. List three (3) examples of food preservation and storage techniques that were developed in the 19th century.

   a. _____

   b. _____

   c. _____

3. What is the reasoning behind the design of each element of the professional chef's uniform?

   a. Neckerchief: _____

   b. Black and white checked trousers: _____

   c. White double-breasted jacket: _____

4. List five (5) types of demographic information that may be helpful to a chef in determining what his/her clientele may desire or need.

   a. _____

   b. _____

   c. _____

   d. _____

   e. _____

5. List three (3) ways a professional chef can show pride in performing his/her job.

   a. _____

   b. _____

   c. _____

C. Defining Professionalism

A student chef should try to develop six basic attributes in readiness for his/her role as a professional chef. Fill in the blank with the term that best matches the definition given on the right. (Term choices: knowledge, skill, taste, judgment, dedication, and pride)

Term	**Definition**
1. _____	The ability to make sound decisions such as what items to include on the menu; what, how much, and when to order food; and approving finished items for service; all of which can only be learned through experience.
2. _____	The desire to continually strive for the utmost professionalism and quality in spite of the physical and psychological strains of being a chef.
3. _____	A chef's ability to prepare flavorful and attractive foods that appeal to all senses and to the desires of his/her clientele.
4. _____	The desire to show high self esteem for one's personal and professional accomplishments by means of such details as professional appearance and behavior.

5. _____ An ability developed through practical, hands-on experience that can only be perfected with extended experience.

6. _____ The understanding of a base of information that enables a chef to perform each aspect of the job.

D. Matching

Match each of the terms in List A with the appropriate duty/responsibility in List B. Each choice in List B can only be used once.

	List A	*List B*
_____	1. Saucier	a. Sautéed items and most sauces
_____	2. Friturier	b. Chocolate éclairs
_____	3. Potager	c. Caesar salad
_____	4. Garde Manger	d. Poached sole with caper sauce
_____	5. Rotisseur	e. Veal stock
_____	6. Poissonier	f. Grilled veal tenderloin with black bean sauce
_____	7. Patissier	g. Roast pork with apple chutney
_____	8. Grillardin	h. Ground beef
_____	9. Boucher	j. French fries
_____	10. Boulanger	k. Steamed asparagus with hollandaise sauce
		l. French bread

1F. Chapter Review

For each question below circle either True or False to indicate the correct answer.

1. Aside from quickly preparing foods to order, a *short order cook* may serve much the same role as a tournant, having mastered many cooking stations.
   True   False

2. Today most well run foodservice operations use the formal kitchen brigade system as the means for organizing the kitchen staff.
   True   False

3. Most new concerns that affect the foodservice industry, such as nutrition and sanitation, are brought about by the government.
   True   False

4. It was not until the early 1900's that advances in transportation efficiency improved to the point where the foodservice industry finally began to expand.
   True   False

5. A regional cuisine is one that represents a group of people having common cultural heritage.
   True   False

6. The biggest difference between establishments serving buffets is that restaurants charge by the dish whereas cafeterias charge by the meal.
   True   False

7. The process of cooking can be described as transferring energy from the heat source to the food to alter the food's molecular structure.
   True   False

8. Most consumers choose a restaurant or foodservice establishment because it provides quality service and food for a price they are willing to pay.
   True   False

9. Escoffier is credited with developing the kitchen brigade system used in large restaurant kitchens.
   True   False

10. Although sun-drying, salting, smoking, pickling, and fermenting are effective means of preserving foods, they were passed up for newer technologies due to the labor intensity of preparation.
    True   False

11. As chefs of classical cuisine, it can be said that Carême, Point, and Escoffier also practiced *gastronomy*.
    True   False

12. Dining in the European or Western style by proceeding through a meal course by course, enables diners to simultaneously satisfy all five major groups of taste: sweet, salty, bitter, sour, and spicy.
    True   False

CHAPTER 2

*F*OOD *S*AFETY AND *S*ANITATION

*T*EST *Y*OUR *K*NOWLEDGE

The practice sets provided below have been designed to test your comprehension of the information found in this chapter. It is recommended that you read this chapter completely before attempting these questions.

2A. Terminology

Fill in the blank spaces with the correct definition.

1. Clean _____

2. Cross contamination _____

3. Intoxication _____

4. Microorganisms _____

5. Pathogenic bacteria _____

6. Atmosphere _____

7. Infection _____

8. Acid/alkali balance _____

9. Direct contamination _____

10. Potentially hazardous foods _____

11. Toxin-mediated infection _____

12. Trichinosis _____

13. Temperature danger zone
    (TDZ) _____

14. Virus _____

15. Parasites _____

16. Anisakiasis _____

2B. Multiple Choice

For each question below, choose the one response that correctly answers the question.

1. Which of the following is *not* a necessity for bacteria to survive and reproduce?
   a. Food
   b. Time
   c. Moisture
   d. Sunlight

2. The federal government enacted legislation designed to reduce hazards in the work area and therefore reduce accidents. This legislation is called:
   a. Safe Jobs for Working Americans Act (SJWAA)
   b. Occupational Hazards Prevention Policy (OHPP)
   c. Safety and Health for Working Americans (SHWA)
   d. Occupational Safety and Health Act (OSHA)

3. Which of the following is *not* an important step in proper hand washing?
   a. Use hot running water to thoroughly wet hands and forearms
   b. Apply antibacterial soap and rub hands and arms briskly with lather for at least 10 seconds
   c. Scrub between fingers and under nails with a nail brush
   d. Rinse thoroughly with hot running water
   e. Reapply soap and scrub hands and forearms for another 5-10 seconds, then rinse again in hot water.

4. Choose the statement that accurately describes how frozen foods should be defrosted. Pull the product from the freezer and:
   a. microwave on high in a plastic pan deep enough to catch the moisture.
   b. thaw at room temperature in a pan deep enough to catch the moisture.
   c. thaw in a warming oven on a roasting rack.
   d. thaw under refrigeration in a pan deep enough to catch the moisture.

5. Foods that are considered acidic have a ph that is:
   a. at 7.0
   b. 8.5-10.0
   c. 0-below 7.0
   d. 10.0-14.0

6. Which statement is *false* regarding the HACCP system?
   a. It focuses on the flow of food through the food service facility.
   b. It is a rigorous system of sanitary inspection conducted by the Health Department.
   c. It is an effective and efficient method for managing and maintaining sanitary conditions in a food service operation.
   d. It is a system that should be followed on a daily basis.

2C. Chapter Review

For each question below circle either True or False to indicate the correct answer.

1. The time-temperature principle is one of the best rules to follow to control the growth of bacteria.
   True   False

2. The first thing that should be done when a pest infestation is discovered is to try to find the source.
   True   False

3. A contaminated food will have an unusual odor.
   True   False

4. When cooling semisolid foods, they may be placed in any size container providing they are refrigerated at 40°F (4°C) or below.
   True   False

5. Food handlers are a major cause for the spread of bacteria.
   True   False

6. A dish can be clean without being sanitary.
   True   False

7. The acronym HACCP stands for Hazard Analysis Critical Control Points.
   True   False

8. Vinyl or plastic gloves are important to food handlers because they eliminate the need to wash hands frequently.
   True   False

9. Hepatitis A is a parasite that often enters shellfish through polluted waters, is carried by humans, and is often transmitted either by cross contamination or by infected food handlers practicing poor personal hygiene.
   True   False

10. The high internal temperatures reached during cooking (165°F-212°F/74°C-100°C) kill most of the bacteria than can cause food-borne illnesses.
    True   False

2D. Food-Borne Diseases Review

This section provides a review of information regarding food-borne diseases. Fill in the blanks provided with the response that correctly completes each portion of the statement. Below is a definition of each of the points needing answers for each question.

Organism:	What type of organism causes the disease? Is it a bacteria, parasite, virus, fungi, mold, or yeast?
Form:	Especially relevant to bacteria, what form does it take? Is it a cell, a toxin, or a spore?
Source:	In what foods might this organism be found, or what is the source of the contaminant?
Prevention:	How can an outbreak of this disease be avoided?

1. *Botulism*

   Organism: _____

   Form: _____

   Source: _____

   Prevention: _____

2. *Hepatitis A*

   Organism: _____

   Source: _____

   Prevention: _____

3. *Strep*

   Organism: _____

   Form: _____

   Source: _____

   Prevention: _____

4. *Perfringens or CP*

   Organism: _____

   Form: _____

   Source: _____

   Prevention: _____

5. *Norwalk Virus*

   Organism: _____

   Source: _____

   Prevention: _____

6. *Salmonella*

   Organism: _____

Form: _____

Source: _____

Prevention: _____

7. *E. Coli or 0157*

   Organism: _____

   Form: _____

   Source: _____

   Prevention: _____

8. *Trichinosis*

   Organism: _____

   Source: _____

   Prevention: _____

9. *Anisakiasis*

   Organism: _____

   Source: _____

   Prevention: _____

10. *Listeriosis*

   Organism: _____

   Form: _____

   Source: _____

   Prevention: _____

11. *Staphylococcus*

   Organism: _____

   Form: _____

   Source: _____

   Prevention: _____

CHAPTER 3

NUTRITION

TEST YOUR KNOWLEDGE

The practice sets provided below have been designed to test your comprehension of the information found in this chapter. It is recommended that you read this chapter completely before attempting these questions.

3A. Terminology

Fill in the blank spaces with the correct definition.

1. Essential nutrients   _____

2. Ingredient alternatives   _____

3. Complex carbohydrates   _____

4. Dietary fiber   _____

5. Calorie   _____

6. Metabolism   _____

7. Ingredient substitutes   _____

8. Simple carbohydrates   _____

3B. The Chef's Role in Nutrition

Fill in the blank provided with the response that correctly completes the statement.

1. List five things a foodservice worker can do to meet the diverse nutritional needs of the consumer.

   a. _____

   b. _____

   c. _____

   d. _____

   e. _____

2. Briefly discuss how you feel a chef should determine what and how many healthful food items should be included on a restaurant menu without limiting or "turning off" other guests.

   _____

   _____

   _____

   _____

   _____

   _____

   _____

   _____

   _____

3. When modifying a recipe, the chef should first identify the ingredient(s) or cooking method(s) that may need to be changed. Once that is done, what three principles should the chef follow to make the dish healthier?

   a. _____

   b. _____

   c. _____

3C. Parts of a Food Label

Identify the six areas of importance on the food label below. Briefly explain the significance of each.

Nutrition Facts

Serving Size ½ cup (114g)
Servings Per Container 4

Amount Per Serving

Calories 90   Calories from Fat 30

% Daily Value*

Total Fat 3g	**5%**
Saturated Fat 0g	**0%**
Cholesterol 0mg	**0%**
Sodium 300mg	**13%**
Total Carbohydrate 13g	**4%**
Dietary Fiber 3g	**12%**
Sugars 3g	
Protein 3g	

Vitamin A	80%	Vitamin C	60%
Calcium	4%	Iron	4%

* Percent Daily Values are based on a 2,000 calorie diet. Your daily values may be higher or lower depending on your calorie needs:

		Calories	2,000	2,500
Total Fat	Less than		65g	80g
Sat Fat	Less than		20g	25g
Cholesterol	Less than		300mg	300mg
Sodium	Less than		2,400mg	2,400mg
Total Carbohydrate			300g	375g
Fiber			25g	30g

Calories per gram:
Fat 9   •   Carbohydrate 4   •   Protein 4

a. _____

b. _____

c. _____

d. _____

e. _____

f. _____

Part of label	Significance
a. _____	_____
b. _____	_____
c. _____	_____
d. _____	_____
e. _____	_____
f. _____	_____

3D. The Food Guide Pyramid

Match each of the terms in *List A* with the appropriate letter in *List B*. Each choice in List B can only be used once.

List A	List B
_____ 1. Fats, oils, sweets	a. 1992
_____ 2. Bread, cereal, rice and pasta group	b. Provides vitamins A&C, Potassium, fiber
_____ 3. Protein	c. Most helpful diet planning tool
_____ 4. 2-3 servings of milk, yogurt and cheese	d. Instituted in 1956, preceding the Pyramid
_____ 5. Food guide pyramid	e. 6-11 servings per day
_____ 6. 2-4 servings of fruit	f. Use sparingly
_____ 7. Vegetable group	g. 3-5 servings per day
_____ 8. Four basic food groups	h. 4-6 servings per day
_____ 9. Food pyramid instituted by USDA	i. Provides calcium, protein, riboflavin
	j. 2-3 servings per day

3E. Essential Nutrients

For each question below, choose the one response that correctly answers the question.

1. Saturated fats are usually solid at room temperature and are found in which of the following food sources?
   a. Fruits, vegetables, grains
   b. Canola and olive oils
   c. Corn, cottonseed, sunflower and safflower oils
   d. Milk, eggs, meats and other foods from animal sources

2. Which one of the following statements is *true* about water?
   a. The average adult should consume at least 4-6 glasses of water a day
   b. Water is necessary for transporting nutrients and wastes
   c. Water is necessary to maintain the proper viscosity and flow of blood
   c. The human body is approximately 80% water

3. Which of the following statements is *false* about complex carbohydrates?
   a. They are naturally occurring in sugars in fruit, vegetables and milk
   b. Fiber is a complex carbohydrate that cannot be digested
   c. Complex carbohydrates are digested into glucose
   d. Starch is a complex carbohydrate

4. Which of the following is *false* about vitamins? They are:
   a. vital dietary substances needed to regulate metabolism
   b. can be divided into two categories: fat soluble and water soluble
   c. necessary for manufacturing, maintaining and repairing body tissue
   d. non-caloric and needed in small amounts

3F. Chapter Review

For each question below circle either True or False to indicate the correct answer.

1. Restauranteurs are required to supply nutrition information only if they make a claim about a specific dish.
   True   False

2. RDA stands for *Recommended Daily Allowances*.
   True   False

3. A food that is labeled as 100% organic must be grown and manufactured without the use of added hormones, pesticides, or synthetic fertilizers. It is regulated by the USDA.
   True   False

4. Food processing and preparation can reduce a food's mineral content.
   True   False

5. Carbohydrates, proteins, and fats can be categorized as energy nutrients.
   True   False

6. A chef's moral and primary responsibility as a foodservice professional is to prepare and serve food that meets or exceeds the guidelines set forth by the Food Guide Pyramid.
   True   False

7. Dietary cholesterol can be found in foods from both plant and animal sources.
   True   False

8. The body has more difficulty breaking down polyunsaturated fats.
   True   False

9. Only 9 of the 20 amino acids are essential.
   True   False

10. Any artificial sweetener can be substituted for sugar when preparing baked goods.
    True   False

CHAPTER 4

MENU PLANNING AND FOOD COSTING

TEST YOUR KNOWLEDGE

The practice sets provided below have been designed to test your comprehension of the information found in this chapter. It is recommended that you read this chapter completely before attempting these questions.

4A. Terminology

Fill in the blank spaces with the correct definition.

1. Entree _____

2. Static menu _____

3. Cycle menu _____

4. Market menu _____

5. Hybrid menu _____

6. A la carte _____

7. Semi a la carte _____

8. Table d'hote / Prix fixe _____

9. Recipe _____

10. Standardized recipe _____

11. Weight _____

12. Volume _____

13. Count _____

14. U.S. system _____

15. Metric system _____

16. Yield _____

17. Conversion factor _____

18. As-purchased costs _____

19. Unit costs or prices _____

20. Total recipe cost _____

21. Cost per portion _____

22. Parstock _____

4B. Units of Measure

Fill in the blanks for the following conversions.

1. 1 lb   =   _____ oz

2. 1 oz   =   _____ g

3. 1 lb   =   _____ g   =   _____ kg

4. 1 kg   =   _____ g

5. 1 g   =   _____ oz

6. 1 kg   =   _____ oz   =   _____ lb

7. 1 c   =   _____ tbsp   =   _____ fl oz

8. 2 pt   =   _____ qt   =   _____ fl oz

9. 2 qt   =   _____ gal   =   _____ pt

10. 2 c   =   _____ pt   =   _____ fl oz

4C. Recipe Conversion

The following recipe presently yields 32 6-oz portions. Calculate the conversion factors and convert the quantities in the recipe to yield 28 6-oz portions and 84 3-oz portions.

   NOTE: Remember to convert new yields back into pounds, ounces and quarts or cups.

Cream of Broccoli Soup

	Old Yield 6 qt. (6 lt) 32 Portions 6 oz each	Conversion Factor I	New Yield I 28 Portions 6 oz each	Conversion Factor II	New Yield II 84 Portions 3 oz each
		_____	_____	_____	_____
Butter	3 ½ oz		_____		_____
Onion	12 oz		_____		_____
Celery	2 ½ oz		_____		_____
Broccoli	3 lb		_____		_____
Chicken veloute	4 qt		_____		_____
Chicken stock	2 qt		_____		_____
Heavy cream	24 oz		_____		_____
Broccoli florets	8 oz		_____		_____

4D. Conversion Problems

When making large recipe changes some additional problems may occur. Give a brief description of each problem.

1. Equipment _____

2. Evaporation _____

3. Recipe errors _____

4. Time _____

4E. Unit Costs

1. One case of milk costs $38.25. There are nine (9) half gallons in each case. How much does one cup cost?
   Answer: $_____
2. One case of English muffins cost $18.00. There are six (6) packages of twelve (12) in each case. How much does one (1) muffin cost?
   Answer: $_____

3. One case of olive oil costs $78.00. There are six (6) gallons per case. How much does one quart cost?
Answer: $_____

4. 5 pounds of sliced American cheese cost $12.00. If one slice weighs half an ounce, how much do two slices cost?
Answer: $_____

4F. Cost per Portion

1. Sandwich sales for one week are $1,462.50 and 325 sandwiches are sold. How much does each sandwich cost?
Answer: $_____

2. New England boiled dinner recipe costs are: potatoes - $15.75, carrots - $12.25, turnips - $10.60, cabbage - $9.85, corned beef - $75.50. The employee salaries are $150.00. Thirty dinners are sold. What is the cost per dinner?
Answer: $_____

3. One dozen eggs cost $1.00 and the buffet uses 3 eggs per omelet. How much does one omelet cost?
Answer: $_____

4. In one day a restaurant sells 68 bowls of soup. The total cost is $51.00. What is the cost per bowl of soup?
Answer: $_____

4G. Controlling Food Cost

Briefly describe the impact the following areas have on the operational costs of a restaurant:

1. Menu _____

2. Purchasing _____

3. Receiving _____

4. Storing _____

5. Issuing _____

6. Standard portions _____

7. Waste _____

8. Sales & service _____

CHAPTER 5

TOOLS AND EQUIPMENT

TEST YOUR KNOWLEDGE

The practice sets provided below have been designed to test your comprehension of the information found in this chapter. It is recommended that you read this chapter completely before attempting these questions.

5A. Terminology

Fill in the blank spaces with the correct definition.

1. Carbon steel   _____

2. Stainless steel   _____

3. High carbon stainless steel _____

. 4 Bird's beak knife   _____

5. Scimitar   _____

6. Whetstone   _____

7. Vertical cutter/mixer   _____

8. Flat top   _____

9. Griddles   _____

10. Salamander   _____

11. Rotisserie   _____

12. Insulated carriers   _____

13. Chafing dishes _____

14. Heat lamps _____

15. Work stations _____

16. Work sections _____

5B. Equipment Identification

Identify each of the following items and give a use for each.

Hand Tools:

1. Name of item: _____Zesta_____
   Major use: _____Donish_____
   _____

2. Name of item: _____cote spatula_____
   Major use: _____Icing_____
   _____

3. Name of item: _____off set_____
   Major use: _____Saute_____
   _____

24

4. Name of item: __Meat Mallot__

   Major use: _____

   _____

5. Name of item: __Chef Fork__

   Major use: _____

   _____

Knives:

6. Name of item: __Chef Knive__

   Major use: _____

   _____

7. Name of item: __Boning Knive__

   Major use: __Cutting fruits and vegles__

   _____

8. Name of item: __Rearing Knive__

   Major use: _____

   _____

9. Name of item: _Bread Knive_

Major use: _____

_____

10. Name of item: _Butcher Knive_

Major use: _Slice Pork chops_

_____

11. Name of item: _Steel_

Major use: _____

_____

Cookware:

12. Name of item: _Stock Pot_

Major use: _Stocks, chicken, vegies_

_____

13. Name of item: _____RONDEAU_____
    Major use: _____Stew_____
    _____

14. Name of item: _____Sautoir_____
    Major use: _____Stew, Braising_____
    _____

15. Name of item: _____Saute PAN_____
    Major use: _____Saute vegies_____
    _____Pan frie_____

16. Name of item: _____WOK_____
    Major use: _____Stir fries_____

17. Name of item: _____Hotel PAN_____
    Major use: _____Hot Holding_____

18. Name of item: _____TAMIS_____
    Major use: _____sifts_____

19. Name of item: _Chinois_

    Major use: _Straining Sauces and soups_

20. Name of item: _Skimmer_

    Major use: _skims tops_

21. Name of item: _Spider_

    Major use: _Scouping_

22. Name of item: _Food Mill_

    Major use: _Puree_

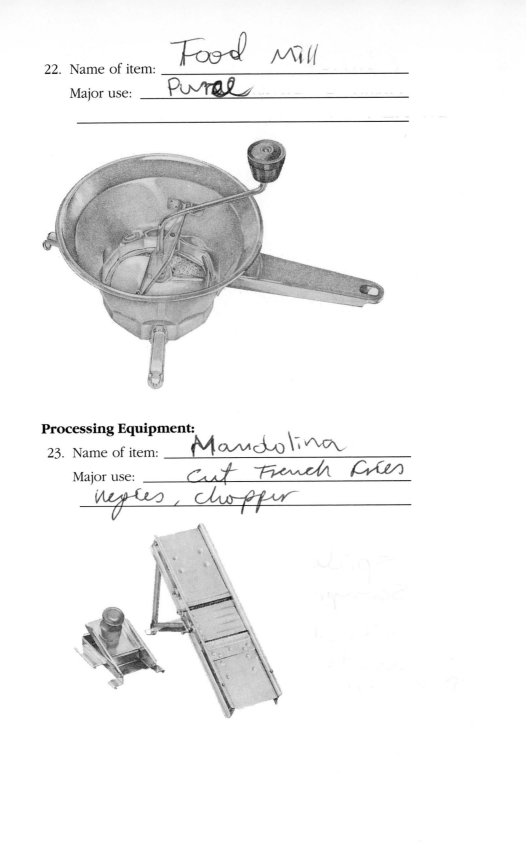

Processing Equipment:

23. Name of item: _Mandolina_

    Major use: _Cut French fries_
    vegies, chopper

24. Name of item: _Blender_

 Major use: _____

 _____

Heavy Equipment:

25. Name of item: _PIZZA OVEN_

 Major use: _____

 _____

26. Name of item: _____

    Major use: _____

    _____

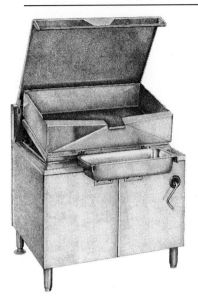

27. Name of item: _____

    Major use: _____

    _____

28. Name of item: _____

     Major use: _____

     _____

29. Name of item: _____

     Major use: _____

     _____

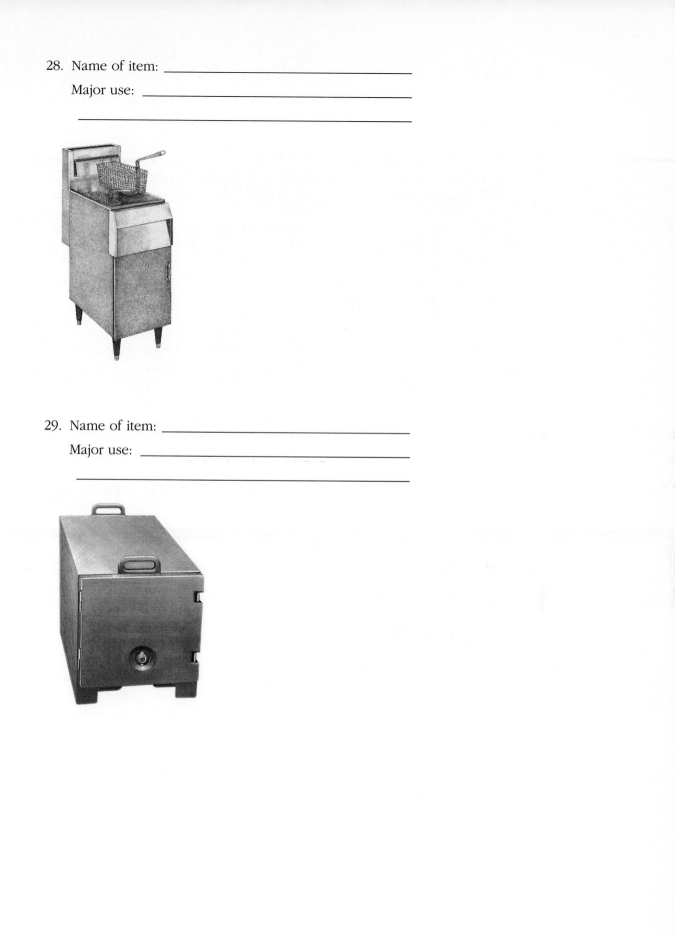

5C. Matching

Match each of the pieces of equipment in List A with the appropriate letter definition in List B. Each choice in List B can only be used once.

	List A	**List B**
_____	1. Mandolin	a. Can be used in food up to 400° F (204° C).
_____	2. Refrigerator	b. The metal used most commonly for knife blades.
_____	3. Candy thermometer	c. A metal that holds and distributes heat very well but is quite heavy.
_____	4. Salamander	d. Food is placed on a revolving spit.
_____	5. Copperware	e. An overhead broiler used to brown the top of foods.
_____	6. Rotisserie	f. A loosely woven cotton fabric used to strain sauces and stocks.
_____	7. Cast iron	g. The metal which is the most effective conductor of heat for cookware.
_____	8. Cheesecloth	h. Used for food storage, may be walk-in or reach-in.
_____	9. Tilting skillet	i. A manually operated slicer used for small quantities of fruit and vegetables.
_____	10. Aluminum	j. A piece of equipment that can be used for frying or braising.
		k. A metal that changes color when in contact with acid foods.

5D. Short Answer

Provide a short response that correctly answers each of the questions below.

1. List three (3) of the six (6) requirements for NSF certification of kitchen tools and equipment.

   a. _____

   b. _____

   c. _____

2. Describe four (4) important criteria for evaluation of equipment for kitchen use.

   a. _____

   b. _____

   c. _____

   d. _____

3. List and describe the three (3) types of metals used in knife blades.

   a. _____

   b. _____

   c. _____

5E. Fill in the Blank

Fill in the blank with the response that correctly completes the statement.

1. A _____ knife is used for general purpose cutting of fruits and vegetables.
2. The part of the knife known as the _____ is the part of the blade that is inside the handle.
3. Short-order and fast-food operations often use a flat metal surface known as a _____ on which to cook food.
4. A _____ _____ is useful for chopping large quantities of foods to a uniform size.
5. It is advisable to use _____ spoons when cooking with nonstick surfaces.
6. A butcher knife is also known as a _____.

5F. Calibrating a Stem-Type Thermometer

Describe the four (4) basic steps required to calibrate a stem-type thermometer:

1. _____

   _____

2. _____

   _____

3. _____

   _____

4. _____

   _____

5G. Chapter Review

For each question below circle either True or False to indicate the correct answer.

1. Stem-type thermometers should be thrown away when they are dropped.
   True   False

2. Ventilation hoods should be cleaned and inspected by the hotel/restaurant maintenance staff.
   True   False

3. Some hand-made imported pottery may contain lead in the glaze.
   True   False

4. Class A fire extinguishers are used for fires caused by wood, paper, or cloth.
   True   False

5. High carbon stainless steel discolors when it comes in contact with acidic foods.
   True   False

6. A steam kettle cooks more slowly than a pot sitting on a stove.
   True   False

CHAPTER 6

*K*NIFE *S*KILLS

*T*EST *Y*OUR *K*NOWLEDGE

The practice sets provided below have been designed to test your comprehension of the information found in this chapter. It is recommended that you read the chapter completely before attempting these questions.

6A. Terminology

Fill in the blank spaces with the correct definition.

1. Whetstone _____

2. Steel _____

3. Chiffonade _____

4. Rondelles / rounds _____

5. Diagonals _____

6. Oblique or roll-cut _____

7. Lozenges _____

8. Butterfly _____

9. Julienne _____

10. Batonnet _____

11. Brunoise _____

12. Small dice _____

13. Medium dice _____

14. Large dice _____

15. Payasanne _____

16. Gaufrette _____

6B. Knife Safety

Briefly describe the eight (8) basic steps for knife safety.

1. _____

_____

2. _____

_____

3. _____

_____

4. _____

_____

5. _____

_____

6. _____

_____

7. _____

_____

8. _____

_____

6C. Cuts of Vegetables

Draw the following cuts of vegetables to scale and describe their dimensions. Point out any similarities between the strips of vegetables and the cubes in the space provided below.

_____

_____

_____

1. Julienne   4. Brunoise

2. Batonnet   5. Small dice

3. Paysanne   6. Medium dice

6D. Fill in the Blank

Fill in the blank with the response that correctly completes the statement.

1. There are _____ methods of cutting, one where the _____ acts as the fulcrum and the other where the _____ acts as the fulcrum.
2. Parsley and garlic should be chopped with one hand flat on the _____ of the knife, using a _____ motion.
3. When cutting food always cut _____ from yourself and never cut on _____, _____, or _____ surfaces.
4. When using a whetstone, start by placing the _____ of the knife on the stone. Start sharpening on the _____ side of the stone and finish with the _____ side.
5. An onion is diced by cutting it in half and then making incisions toward the _____ of the onion, without cutting through it.

6E. Dicing an Onion

Describe the five (5) steps necessary to dice an onion.

1. _____

   _____

2. _____

   _____

3. _____

   _____

4. _____

   _____

5. _____

   _____

6F. Chapter Review

For each question below circle either True or False to indicate the correct answer.

1. A sharp knife is more dangerous than a dull one.
   True   False

2. Tourner means "to turn" in French.
   True   False

3. A steel is used to sharpen knives.
   True   False

4. Batonnet are also referred to as allumette.
   True   False

5. A whetstone should be moistened with a mixture of water and mineral oil.
   True   False

6. Paysanne is a half-inch dice that has been cut in half.
   True   False

7. One should not attempt to catch a falling knife.
   True   False

8. Knives should not be washed in the dishwasher.
   True   False

CHAPTER 7

*K*ITCHEN *S*TAPLES

*T*EST *Y*OUR *K*NOWLEDGE

The practice sets provided below have been designed to test your comprehension of the information found in this chapter. It is recommended that you read the chapter completely before attempting these questions.

7A. *Terminology*

Fill in the blank spaces with the correct term.

1. Onion piquet _____

2. Herbs _____

3. Table salt _____

4. Nuts _____

5. Shortenings _____

6. Spices _____

7. Vinegar _____

8. Smoke point _____

9. Pickles _____

10. Flavorings _____

11. Rancid _____

12. Relish _____

7B. Categorizing Flavorings

Based on the two categories given, identify the items from the list below that are examples of each category. Fill in the blanks provided under each category heading with the corresponding examples.

Herb	**Spice**
1. _____	6. _____
2. _____	7. _____
3. _____	8. _____
4. _____	9. _____
5. _____	10. _____

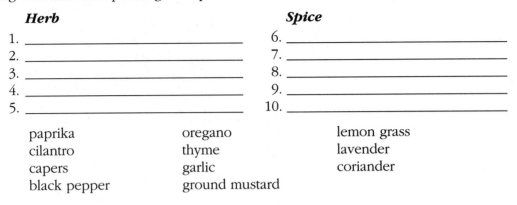

paprika	oregano	lemon grass
cilantro	thyme	lavender
capers	garlic	coriander
black pepper	ground mustard	

7C. Herbs and Spices

For each question below, choose the one response that correctly answers the question.

1. Which of the following is *not* one of the three guidelines to follow when experimenting with the use of different herbs and spices in various dishes?
   a. Flavorings should be added at the beginning of the preparation.
   b. Flavorings should not hide the taste or aroma of the primary ingredients.
   c. Flavorings should be combined in balance, so as not to overwhelm the palate.
   d. Flavorings should not be used to disguise poor quality or poorly prepared products.

2. Which spice does the following description identify?
   Thin layers of bark that are peeled from branches of small evergreen trees and dried in the sun. This pale brown spice is most commonly purchased ground since it is difficult to grind.
   a. Nutmeg
   b. Allspice
   c. Cinnamon
   d. Mace

3. Which spice does the following description identify?
   Hand-picked, dried stigmas of a type of crocus that are the most expensive spice in the world.
   a. Turmeric
   b. Saffron
   c. Poppy seeds
   d. Juniper

4. Which herb does the following description identify?
   Hollow, thin, grass-like stems that have a mild onion flavor and bright green color.
   a. Chervil
   b. Lemon grass
   c. Dill
   d. Chives

5. Which herb does the following description identify?
   A flowering herb commonly used as a flavoring in Mediterranean cooking and having a flavor similar to thyme, only sweeter. The wild version of this herb is known as oregano.
   a. Cilantro
   b. Lemon thyme
   c. Rosemary
   d. Marjoram

6. Which spice does the following description identify?
   Round and beige seeds from the cilantro plant that have a sweet, spicy flavor and strong aroma.
   a. Coriander
   b. Cardamom
   c. Fenugreek
   d. Cumin

7. Which spice does the following description identify?
   A root that comes from a tall, flowering tropical plant and has a fiery yet sweet flavor, with hints of lemon and rosemary. It is used extensively in Asian cookery.
   a. Turmeric
   b. Cloves
   c. Ginger
   d. Caraway

8. Which herb does the following description identify?
   Commonly used in Mediterranean cuisines, it has a strong, warm and slightly peppery flavor with a hint of cloves. It is available in a variety of "flavors"—cinnamon, garlic, lemon and chocolate.
   a. Garlic chives
   b. Sweet basil
   c. Rosemary
   d. Oregano

9. Which herb does the following description identify?
   Typically used in poultry dishes, with fatty meats or brewed as a beverage, its strong balsamic/camphor flavor does not blend well with other herbs.
   a. Savory
   b. Tarragon
   c. Thyme
   d. Sage

10. Which herb does the following description identify?
    A member of the parsley family that has delicate blue-green, feathery leaves and whose flavor is similar to parsley, only with a hint of anise.
    a. Fennel
    b. Dill
    c. Tarragon
    d. Chervil

7D. Coffees and Teas

Fill in the blanks provided with the response that correctly completes the statement.

1. Coffee can be judged on four characteristics:

   a. _____ refers to the feeling of heaviness or thickness that coffee provides on the palate.

   b. _____ will often indicate the taste of coffee.

   c. _____ refers to the tartness of the coffee, lending a snap, life, or thinness.

   d. _____The most ambiguous as well as the most important characteristic, having to do with taste.

2. _____ is a commercial coffee bean from which the finest coffees are produced.

3. _____ is a bean which does not produce as flavorful a coffee, but is becoming more significant commercially since the trees are heartier and more fertile than their predecessors.

4. The best results for brewing a good cup of coffee are nearly always achieved by using _____ level tablespoons of ground coffee per 3/4 measuring cup (_____ ounces) of water.

5. A cup of _____ is often either the very first or the very last item consumed by a customer.

6. _____, whether iced or hot, is often consumed throughout the meal.

7. _____, _____, and _____ are the 3 basic types of tea.

7E. Chapter Review

For each question below, circle either True or False to indicate the correct answer.

1. Green tea is yellow-green in color and partially fermented to release its characteristics.
   True   False

2. Ketchup originally referred to any salty extract from fish, fruits, or vegetables.
   True   False

3. In reference to making beverages, the term steeping means mixing hot water with the ground coffee.
   True   False

4. When preparing a recipe that calls for fresh herbs, the rule to follow when fresh herbs are unavailable is: use more dried herbs than the original fresh variety.
   True   False

5. A standard sachet consists of peppercorns, bay leaves, parsley stems, thyme, cloves, and optionally garlic.
   True   False

6. Mustard never really spoils, its flavor just fades away.
   True   False

7. The real definition of a nut is the edible single-seed kernel of a fruit surrounded by a hard shell.
   True   False

8. Café latte is made by mixing 1/4 espresso with 3/4 steamed milk without foam.
   True   False

9. Whole coffee beans will stay fresh for a few weeks at room temperature whereas ground coffee will only stay fresh three or four days.
   True   False

10. Vegetable oils are cholesterol free, are virtually odorless, and have a neutral flavor.
    True   False

11. Olive oil is extracted from a fruit.
    True   False

12. Distilled vinegar is made from white wine and is completely clear with a stronger vinegar flavor and higher acid content than most vinegars.
    True   False

13. Salt is used as a basic seasoning universally and its flavor can be tasted and smelled easily.
    True   False

14. Every culture tends to combine a small number of flavoring ingredients so frequently and so consistently that they become a definite part of that particular cuisine.
    True   False

CHAPTER 8

DAIRY PRODUCTS

TEST YOUR KNOWLEDGE

The practice sets provided below have been designed to test your comprehension of the information found in this chapter. It is recommended that you read the chapter completely before attempting these questions.

8A. Terminology

Fill in the blank spaces with the correct definition.

1. Cream cheese   _____

2. Heavy whipping cream   _____

3. Fondue   _____

4. Dairy products   _____

5. Non-fat milk   _____

6. Half-and-half cream   _____

7. Whipped butter   _____

8. Skim milk   _____

9. Buttermilk   _____

10. Salted butter   _____

11. Lowfat milk   _____

12. Yogurt   _____

13. Light cream   _____

14. Sour cream   _____

8B. Comparing Creams

Match each type of cream in List A with the appropriate fat content in List B.

Cream

_____ 1. light whipping
_____ 2. light cream
_____ 3. half and half
_____ 4. heavy (whipping) cream

Fat content

a. not less than 36% milkfat
b. 10%–18% milkfat
c. 16%–23% milkfat
d. 18%–less than 30% milkfat
e. 30%–36% milkfat

8C. Cheese Identification

Match each of the cheese varieties in List A with the appropriate letter definition in List B.

List A

_____ 1. Mozzarella

_____ 2. American cheddar

_____ 3. Parmigiano-Reggiano

_____ 4. Gruyère

_____ 5. Boursin

_____ 6. Roquefort

_____ 7. Chevre

_____ 8. Brie

_____ 9. Feta

_____ 10. Havarti

_____ 11. Ricotta

_____ 12. Monterey jack

List B

a. French, semi-soft, blue-veined sheep's milk cheese containing 45 % fat.

b. A hard, cow's milk cheese containing from 32% to 35% fat and produced exclusively near Parma, Italy.

c. A cheddar-like cow's milk cheese from California containing 50% fat.

d. A fresh, soft Italian cow's milk cheese similar to cottage cheese containing 4%-10% fat.

e. A fresh, firm, Italian cow's milk cheese very mild in flavor, and can become elastic when cooked.

f. A French, rindless, soft, triple cream cow's milk cheese usually flavored with garlic, herbs, or peppers.

g. A firm, cow's milk cheese made primarily in NY, WI, VT, and OR, 45% to 50% fat.

h. A well-known, mild Wisconsin cheddar containing from 45%-50% fat.

i. A sharp-flavored, hard sheep's milk cheese from Central and Southern Italy containing 35% fat.

j. A milder, French or Belgian soft rind-ripened cheese made from cow's milk, containing 45% fat.

k. A semi-soft cow's-milk cheese from Piedmont, Italy containing 45% fat.

l. A soft, French, rind-ripened cheese made with cow's milk and containing 60% fat.

_____ 13. Gorgonzola

_____ 14. Mascarpone

_____ 15. Colby

_____ 16. Camembert

_____ 17. Pecorino-Romano

m. A firm, Swiss, cow's milk cheese that is highly flavorful, sweet and nutty, and aged up to 12 months.

n. A fresh, soft, Italian cow's milk cheese originally from Lombardy, Italy containing 70%-75% fat.

o. A fresh, soft, American cow's milk cheese containing 35% fat.

p. A semi-soft, Italian, blue-veined cow's milk cheese containing 48% fat.

q. A pale yellow, Danish cow's milk cheese with many small, irregular holes, often made with herbs and spices.

r. A fresh, Italian or Greek sheep and/or goat's milk cheese that is white and flaky, from pickling in brine.

s. A soft, creamy, goat's milk cheese with a short shelf life.

8D. Milk Products

For each question below, choose the one response that correctly answers the question.

1. Milk products should be kept refrigerated at or below:
   a. 30°F
   b. 35°F
   c. 40°F
   d. 45°F

2. Aside from increasing the shelf life of cream, the process of ultrapasteurization:
   a. reduces the whipping properties
   b. thickens the consistency
   c. causes the cream to stay whipped for longer periods of time
   d. concentrates the fat content

3. Which one of the following is _false_ regarding concentrated or condensed milk products? They:
   a. do not require refrigeration once opened.
   b. are produced by using a vacuum to remove all or part of the water from whole milk.
   c. have a high concentration of milkfat and milk solids.
   d. have an extended shelf life.

4. Grades of milk are assigned based on:
   a. the clarity of color and distribution of fat globules.
   b. bacterial count; no less than 20 and no more than 30 per gallon earns a grade A.
   c. bacterial count; the lower it is, the higher the grade.
   d. the flavor of the milk as determined by the breed and feed of the animal.

5. Which one of the following is *false* regarding homogenization? It:
   a. breaks the fat globules in the whole milk into a smaller size and permanently disperses them.
   b. is not required but is commonly performed on commercial products.
   c. results in a milk product with a whiter color and richer taste.
   d. increases the shelf life of the milk product.

6. Which of the following is *true* regarding pasteurization? It requires holding the milk at a temperature of:
   a. 140°F for 15 seconds
   b. 161°F for 15 seconds
   c. 275°F for a very short time
   d. 280° to 300° for 2 to 6 seconds

7. Evaporated milk, sweetened condensed milk, and dry milk powders are all examples of:
   a. canned milk products
   b. concentrated milk products
   c. cultured dairy products
   d. substandard milk products

8. Which of the following is *true* about sweetened condensed milk? It:
   a. contains between 60% and 65% sugar.
   b. can be substituted for whole milk or evaporated milk.
   c. is concentrated like evaporated milk by removing 60% of the water.
   d. has a brilliant, white color and faint flavor of caramel.

8E. Chapter Review

For each question below circle either True or False to indicate the correct answer.

1. Milk products processed by ultra high temperature (UHT) processing can be stored without refrigeration for at least three months.
   True   False

2. Margarine contains cholesterol.
   True   False

3. Coffee whiteners, imitation sour cream, and whipped topping mixes are made from nondairy products.
   True   False

4. All grades of milk must be pasteurized before retail sale.
   True   False

5. The lack of moisture in dry milk powder prevents the growth of microorganisms.
   True   False

6. Seasoning butter with salt changes the butter's flavor and extends its shelf life.
   True   False

7. Both butter and margarine contain about 80% fat and 16% water.
   True   False

8. Yogurt is a good example of a health or diet food.
   True   False

9. Margarine is a dairy product that serves as a good substitute to butter.
   True   False

10. Aside from excess moisture, processed cheese foods are of equal quality as natural cheeses.
    True   False

11. One pound of whole butter that is clarified will result in 12 ounces of clarified butter.
    True   False

12. Natural cheeses contain cholesterol.
    True   False

PRINCIPLES OF COOKING

TEST YOUR KNOWLEDGE

The practice sets provided below have been designed to test your comprehension of the information found in this chapter. It is recommended that you read the chapter completely before attempting these questions.

9A. Terminology

Fill in the blank spaces with the correct definition.

1. Convection   _____

2. Coagulation   _____

3. Gelatinization   _____

4. Radiation   _____

5. Conduction   _____

6. Combination cooking methods   _____

7. Mechanical convection   _____

8. Infrared cooking   _____

9. Carmelization   _____

10. Moist heat cooking methods   _____

11. Microwave cooking   _____

12. Evaporates   _____

13. Melt   _____

14. Dry heat cooking methods _____

15. Natural convection   _____

9B. Cooking Methods

Fill in the spaces provided with the response that correctly completes information about each cooking method.

Cooking method	Medium	Equipment
ex: *sautéing*	*fat*	*stove*
1. Stewing	_____	_____
2. Deep-fat frying	_____	_____
3. Broiling	_____	_____
4. Poaching	_____	_____
5. Grilling	_____	_____
6. Simmering	_____	_____
7. Baking	_____	_____
8. Roasting	_____	_____
9. Steaming	_____	_____
10. Braising	_____	_____

9C. Multiple Choice

For each question below, choose the one response that correctly answers the question.

1. Which method refers to the transfer of heat through a fluid?
   a. convection
   b. radiation
   c. conduction
   d. induction

2. What cooking technique is an example of moist cooking?
   a. grilling
   b. sautéing
   c. deep-fat frying
   d. steaming

3. The purpose for the shape of the wok used for stir-frying is that the rounded shape:
   a. makes it easier to pour liquids out of it.
   b. is designed to fit into the specially designed shape of the turbo gas burners.
   c. diffuses the heat and makes tossing and stirring easier.
   d. makes the cookware more durable.

4. Which of the following is an example of infrared cooking?
   a. broiling
   b. sautéing
   c. roasting
   d. baking

5. In pan-frying, how much fat or oil should be in the pan?
   a. Just enough to coat the bottom of the pan
   b. 1 cup measure
   c. 1/2 to 2/3 way up on the product being cooked
   d. Enough to completely cover the product

6. What cooking technique is defined in the following statement: "To briefly and partially cook a food in boiling water or hot liquid"?
   a. boiling
   b. blanching
   c. frying
   d. simmering

7. Which does *not* describe convection heat transfer?
   a. The natural tendency of warm liquids and gases to rise while cooler ones fall.
   b. Fans or a stirring motion circulate heat.
   c. A combination of conduction and a mixing in which molecules in a fluid (air, water or fat) move from a warmer area to a cooler area.
   d. Energy is transferred by waves of heat or light striking the food.

8. A liquid, thickened with a starch, will begin to thicken gradually (depending on what starch was used) over what temperature range?
   a. 100°F to 130°F
   b. 135°F to 150°F
   c. 150°F to 212°F
   d. 212°F to 250°F

9D. Short Answer

Provide a short response that correctly answers each of the questions below.

1. List the four (4) major differences between braising and stewing

   Braising   **Stewing**

   a. _____   a. _____

   b. _____   b. _____

   c. _____   c. _____

   d. _____   d. _____

2. List two (2) recommendations on how to steam a food product properly.

   a. _____

   b. _____

3. In five (5) steps explain how properly to sauté a chicken breast.

a. _____

b. _____

c. _____

d. _____

e. _____

4. Describe the six (6) steps necessary for correct poaching of a food item.

a. _____

b. _____

c. _____

d. _____

e. _____

f. _____

9E. Matching

1. Match each of the cooking methods in List A with the appropriate temperature in List B. Each choice in List B may be used only once.

List A

_____ 1. boiling
_____ 2. broiling
_____ 3. simmering
_____ 4. poaching
_____ 5. steaming
_____ 6. deep-fat frying

List B

a. 160° F to 180° F
b. 185° F to 205° F
c. up to 2000° F
d. 212° or higher (at sea level)
e. 212° F (at sea level)
f. 212° F to 220° F
g. 325° F to 375° F

9F. Chapter Review

For each question below circle either True or False to indicate the correct answer.

1. In induction cooking the heat energy is transferred from the cookware to the food by conduction.
   True   False

2. A microwave oven can be considered an acceptable replacement for traditional ovens.
   True   False

3. Sautéing is an example of the conduction heat transfer method.
   True   False

4. A wood fired grill is an example of the convection heat transfer method.
   True   False

5. If a pan of sautéing onions is covered with a lid during the cooking process, it becomes a moist-heat cooking method.
   True   False

6. In broiling the heat source comes from below the cooking surface.
   True   False

7. Deep frying is an example of a combination cooking method.
   True   False

8. When creating crosshatch markings on a grilled steak, the meat should be rotated 90 degrees from the original position on the grill.
   True   False

9. Stir-frying is a variation in technique to sauteing except it utilizes more fat in the process.
   True   False

10. A court bouillon should be used when steaming foods to prevent flavor loss.
    True   False

11. Blanching means to partially cook a food product in a boiling liquid or hot fat.
    True   False

12. The process of stewing generally takes less time than braising because the food products are cut into smaller pieces.
    True   False

CHAPTER 10

STOCKS AND SAUCES

TEST YOUR KNOWLEDGE

The practice sets provided below have been designed to test your comprehension of the information found in this chapter. It is recommended that you read the chapter completely before attempting these questions.

10A. Terminology

Fill in the blank spaces with the correct definition.

1. Stock _____

2. Sauce _____

3. White stock _____

4. Brown stock _____

5. Fish stock _____

6. Fumet _____

7. Court bouillon _____

8. Mirepoix _____

9. Cartilage _____

10. Connective tissue _____

11. Collagen _____

12. Gelatin _____

13. Degrease _____

14. Deglaze _____

15. Remouillage _____

16. Sweat _____

17. Mother or leading sauces _____

18. Small or compound
    sauces _____

19. Coulis _____

20. Beurre blanc and beurre
    rouge _____

21. White roux _____

22. Blond roux _____

23. Brown roux _____

24. Slurry _____

25. Tempering _____

26. Reduction _____

27. Bechamel _____

28. Mornay sauce _____

29. Veloute _____

30. Espagnole _____

31. Demi-glace _____

32. Chasseur sauce _____

33. Jus lie _____

34. Gastrique _____

35. Hollandaise sauce _____

36. Bearnaise _____

37. Glacage _____

38. Beurre noir and beurre noisette _____

39. Maitre d'Hotel _____

40. Pan gravy _____

41. Chutney _____

42. Essence, au jus or nage _____

43. Flavored oil _____

44. Pesto _____

10B. Stock-Making Review

Stock-making is a fundamental skill. The procedure for making basic stocks should be second nature to all good chefs.

List the essential ingredients and describe in a step-by-step manner the cooking procedure for white stock, brown stock and fish stock. Exact quantities are not important for this exercise, however, cooking times should be included and each step should be numbered for revision purposes.

White Stock

Ingredients: *Procedure:*

_____

_____

_____

_____

_____

_____

_____

_____

_____

_____

_____

Brown Stock

Ingredients: *Procedure:*

_____

_____

_____

_____

_____

_____

_____

_____

_____

Fish Stock

Ingredients: *Procedure:*

_____

_____

_____

_____

_____

_____

_____

_____

_____

_____

10C. Sauce Review

This section reviews the make-up of the five mother sauces. In the spaces provided below fill in the name of the sauce, the thickener used, and the liquid that forms the base of the sauce. For the sauces that use a roux as a thickener please specify the type of roux used.

	Mother Sauce	*Thickener*	*Liquid*
1.	_____	_____	_____
2.	_____	_____	_____
3.	_____	_____	_____
4.	_____	_____	_____
5.	_____	_____	_____

10D. Small Sauces

For the following small sauces identify the leading sauce that forms its base and list the main ingredients or garnish that distinguish them from the mother sauce.

Small Sauce	*Mother Sauce*	*Ingredients Added*
1. Cream sauce	_____	_____
2. Cheddar sauce	_____	_____
3. Mornay	_____	_____
4. Nantua	_____	_____
5. Soubise	_____	_____
6. Allemande	_____	_____
7. Supreme	_____	_____
8. Bercy	_____	_____
9. Cardinal	_____	_____
10. Normandy	_____	_____
11. Aurora	_____	_____
12. Horseradish	_____	_____
13. Poulette	_____	_____
14. Albufera	_____	_____
15. Hungarian	_____	_____
16. Ivory	_____	_____
17. Bordelaise	_____	_____
18. Chasseur	_____	_____

19. Chateaubriand _____ _____

20. Cherveuil _____ _____

21. Madiera or Port _____ _____

22. Marchand de vin _____ _____

23. Perigeaux _____ _____

24. Piquant _____ _____

25. Poivrade _____ _____

26. Robert _____ _____

27. Creole _____ _____

28. Milanaise _____ _____

29. Spanish _____ _____

30. Bearnaise _____ _____

31. Choron _____ _____

32. Foyot _____ _____

33. Grimrod _____ _____

34. Maltaise _____ _____

35. Mousseline _____ _____

10E. Short Answer

Provide a short response that correctly answers each of the questions below.

1. List the seven (7) principles of stock making.

a. _____

b. _____

c. _____

d. _____

e. _____

f. _____

g. _____

2. Hollandaise Preparation:
In the space below list the essential ingredients and describe in a step-by-step manner the preparation of hollandaise sauce, using the classical method. Exact quantities are important for this exercise, and each step should be numbered for revision purposes.

Ingredients: **Procedure:**

_____

_____

_____

_____

_____

_____

_____

_____

_____

3. **Give five (5) reasons why hollandaise sauce might separate.**

a. _____

b. _____

c. _____

d. _____

e. _____

4. **Provide a brief description of how the following thickening agents are combined with the liquid to form a sauce.**

a. Roux _____

_____

b. Cornstarch_____

_____

c. Arrowroot _____

_____

d. Beurre Manie _____

_____

e. Liaison _____

_____

10F. Matching

Match each of the small sauces in List A with the appropriate mother sauce in List B.

List A	**List B**

A. Cream sauce
B. Maltaise
C. Supreme
D. Bordelaise
E. Creole
F. Mornay
G. Bercy
H. Milanaise
I. Choron
J. Nantua
K. Chasseur
L. Bearnaise
M. Cardinal
N. Robert
O. Spanish

1. Espagnole

   _____
   _____
   _____

2. Hollandaise

   _____
   _____
   _____

3. Bechamel

   _____
   _____
   _____

4. Veloute

   _____
   _____
   _____

5. Tomato

   _____
   _____
   _____

10G. Chapter Review

For each question below, circle either True or False to indicate the correct answer.

1. More roux is needed for dark sauces than for light ones.
   True   False

2. To avoid lumps in sauces, add hot stock to hot roux.
   True   False

3. After adding a liaison to a sauce, simmer for 5 minutes.
   True   False

4. Nappe is a term used to describe the consistency of sauce.
   True   False

5. The combination of water and cornstarch is called slurry.
   True   False

6. A velouté is a roux-based sauce.
   True   False

7. The definition of tempering is the gradual lowering of the temperature of a hot liquid by adding a cold liquid.
   True   False

8. A reduction method is sometimes used to thicken sauces.
   True   False

9. Compound sauces come from small sauces.
   True   False

10. Fish stock needs to simmer for one hour in order to impart flavor.
    True   False

CHAPTER 11

Soups

TEST YOUR KNOWLEDGE

The practice sets provided below have been designed to test your comprehension of the information found in this chapter. It is recommended that you read the chapter completely before attempting these quesitons.

11A. Terminology

Fill in the blank spaces with the correct definition.

1. Broth _____

2. Consomme _____

3. Cream soup _____

4. Puree soup _____

5. Bisque _____

6. Chowder _____

7. Cold soup _____

8. Garnish _____

9. Tomato concasse _____

10. Clearmeat or clarification _____

11. Onion brulee _____

12. Raft _____

13. Render _____

11B. Broth Preparation Review

Briefly describe the six (6) steps in the preparation of a broth.

1. _____
2. _____
3. _____
4. _____
5. _____
6. _____

11C. Consommé Preparation Review I

The procedure for making consomme is time tested. List the essential ingredients and describe the eight (8) steps necessary for the production of consommé.

1. _____
2. _____
3. _____
4. _____
5. _____
6. _____
7. _____
8. _____

11D. Consommé Preparation Review II

Provide a reason for each of the following problems with consommé preparation.

1. Cloudy _____
2. Greasy _____
3. Lacks flavor _____
4. Lacks color _____

11E. Consommé Preparation Review III

Describe the four (4) steps that can be taken to correct a poorly clarified consommé.

1. _____
2. _____
3. _____
4. _____

11F. Cream Soup Preparation Review

List the essential ingredients and describe the seven (7) essential steps for making a cream soup.

1. _____

2. _____

    _____

    _____

    _____

    _____

3. _____

4. _____

5. _____

6. _____

7. _____

11G. Short Answer

Provide a short response that correctly answers each of the questions below.

1. List three (3) steps that can be taken to prevent cream from curdling when it is added to cream soups.

    a. _____

    b. _____

    c. _____

2. List the seven (7) common categories of soups and provide two (2) examples of type. Suggest an appropriate garnish for each soup.

	Soup	**Example**	**Garnish**
a.	_____	_____	_____
		_____	_____
b.	_____	_____	_____
		_____	_____
c.	_____	_____	_____
		_____	_____
d.	_____	_____	_____
		_____	_____
e.	_____	_____	_____
		_____	_____

f. _____ _____ _____

_____ _____

g. _____ _____ _____

_____ _____

3. Compare and contrast the following soups. Explain what they have in common, and what makes them different from one another.

a. Beef broth   Consommé

_____

_____

_____

_____

b. Cream of mushroom   Lentil soup

_____

_____

_____

c. Gazpacho   Cold consommé

_____

_____

_____

_____

11H. Chapter Review

For each question below, circle either True or False to indicate the correct answer.

1. A purée soup is usually more chunky than a cream soup.
   True   False

2. A cream soup is always finished with milk or cream.
   True   False

3. Consommé should be stirred after the clearmeat is added.
   True   False

4. A broth is a consommé with vegetables added to it.
   True   False

5. Cream soups are thickened with a purée of vegetables which have been cooked in a stock.
   True   False

6. French onion soup has only one garnish: the croutons.
   True   False

7. Cold soups should be served at room temperature.
   True   False

8. Once a consommé is clouded it should be discarded.
   True   False

9. Cold soups need less seasoning than hot soups.
   True   False

10. A roux can be used as a thickener for cold soups.
   True   False.

CHAPTER 12

PRINCIPLES OF MEAT COOKERY

TEST YOUR KNOWLEDGE

The practice sets provided below have been designed to test your comprehension of the information found in this chapter. It is recommended that you read the chapter completely before attempting these questions.

12A. Terminology

Fill in the blank spaces with the correct definition.

1. Primal cuts _____

2. Subprimal cuts _____

3. Fabricated cuts _____

4. Marbling _____

5. Subcutaneous fat _____

6. Elastin _____

7. To butcher _____

8. Dress _____

9. Fabricate _____

10. Carve _____

11. Quality grades _____

12. Yield grades _____

13. Vacuum packaging   _____

14. Portion control   _____

15. Freezer burn   _____

16. Carryover cooking   _____

17. Fond   _____

18. Cutlet   _____

19. Scallop   _____

20. Emince   _____

21. Paillard   _____

22. Medallion   _____

23. Mignonette   _____

24. Noisette   _____

25. Chop   _____

26. Brown stew   _____

27. White stew/fricasse   _____

28. Blanquette   _____

12B. Fill in the Blank

Fill in the blank with the response that correctly completes the statement.

1. Dry heat cooking methods are best used for _____ cuts of meat.
2. Once the meat is added to the sauce for stewing, the dish is cooked at a _____ temperature for a _____ time.
3. Very rare meats should feel _____ and have a _____ color; however, well-cooked meats should feel _____ and have a _____ color.
4. Sauté items are sometimes _____ before being placed in the pan.
5. Some _____ cooking occurs when a roast item is removed from the oven. Allowing the meat to rest will help the meat to _____ _____.
6. Covering the exterior surface with fat before cooking is called _____, and inserting strips of fat into the meat is called _____ .

7. Marinating meats adds a distinctive _____ , and breaks down the _____ _____ to help tenderize the meat.

8. Ionizing radiation kills significant amounts of _____ , _____ , and _____ in meat.

9. Dry heat cooking methods are not recommended for _____ cuts of meat, or those high in connective tissue.

10. When carving roasted meats, it is important to carve _____ the grain.

12C. Matching

Match each of the stews in List A with the appropriate description in List B. Each choice in List B can only be used once.

List A	*List B*
_____ 1. Ragout	a. A spicy ragout of ground or diced meat with vegetables, peppers, and sometimes beans.
_____ 2. Goulash	b. A white stew usually made with white meat and garnished with onions and mushrooms.
_____ 3. Blanquette	c. A brown ragout made with root vegetables and lamb.
_____ 4. Fricassee	d. A general term that refers to stews.
_____ 5. Navarin	e. A Hungarian beef stew made with onions and paprika and garnished with potatoes.
	f. A white stew in which the meat is blanched and added to the sauce to finish the cooking process. This stew is finished with a liaison of cream and egg yolks.

12D. Cooking Methods

Provide a short response that correctly answers each of the questions below.

Briefly describe each of the following methods of cooking and provide an example of a cut of meat used in each method.

Cooking Method	*Description*	*Example*
Grilling	_____	_____
Roasting	_____	_____
Sautéing	_____	_____
Pan-frying	_____	_____
Simmering	_____	_____
Braising	_____	_____
Stewing	_____	_____

12E. Chapter Review

For each question below, circle True or False to indicate the correct answer.

1. Fresh meats should be stored at 35–40° F.
   True   False

2. "Green meats" are meats that are allowed to turn moldy.
   True   False

3. Braising and stewing are combination cooking methods.
   True   False

4. The USDA stamp on whole carcasses of meat does not ensure their quality or tenderness.
   True   False

5. USDA choice meat is used in the finest restaurants and hotels.
   True   False

6. Yield grades are used for beef, lamb, and pork.
   True   False

7. Wet aging occurs in a vacuum package.
   True   False

8. During dry aging the meat may develop mold, which adds to the flavor of the meat.
   True   False

9. Under the correct conditions vacuum-packed meat can be held for 2 to 3 months.
   True   False

10. Still air freezing is the most common method of freezing meats in foodservice facilities.
    True   False.

CHAPTER 13

BEEF

TEST YOUR KNOWLEDGE

The practice sets provided below have been designed to test your comprehension of the information found in this chapter. It is recommended that you read the chapter completely before attempting these questions.

13A. Terminology

Fill in the blank spaces with the correct definition.

For each primal cut of Beef listed below, describe the following:
- a.   % of carcass weight
- b.   Bone structure
- c.   Muscle structure
- d.   Cooking processes applied

1. Chuck   _____

    a. _____

    b. _____

    c. _____

    d. _____

2. Brisket & shank   _____

    a. _____

    b. _____

    c. _____

    d. _____

3. Rib _____

    a. _____

    b. _____

    c. _____

    d. _____

4. Short plate _____

    a. _____

    b. _____

    c. _____

    d. _____

5. Short loin _____

    a. _____

    b. _____

    c. _____

    d. _____

6. Sirloin _____

    a. _____

    b. _____

    c. _____

    d. _____

7. Flank _____

    a. _____

    b. _____

    c. _____

    d. _____

8. Round   _____

     a. _____

     b. _____

     c. _____

     d. _____

9. Offal   _____

     a. _____

     b. _____

     c. _____

     d. _____

13B. Primal Cuts of Beef

Identify the primal cuts of beef indicated in the following diagram and write their names in the spaces provided.

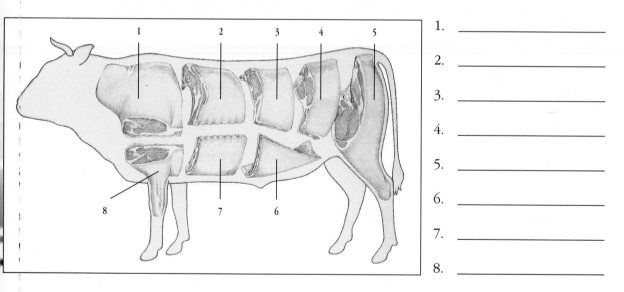

1. _____

2. _____

3. _____

4. _____

5. _____

6. _____

7. _____

8. _____

13C. Cuts from the Round

Name the five (5) subprimal/fabricated cuts from the round and name the most appropriate cooking process or use for each cut.

Subprimal/Fabricated Cut	*Cooking Process/Use*
1. _____	_____
2. _____	_____

3. _____   _____

4. _____   _____

5. _____   _____

13D. Cuts of Beef and Applied Cooking Methods

Name the cooking method applied to the main ingredient in each of the following beef dishes. Also, identify a subprimal and a primal cut of meat from which the main ingredient is taken.

Name of Dish	Cooking Method	Subprimal/ Fabricated Cut	Primal Cut
1. Pot Roast	_____	_____	_____
	_____	_____	_____
2. Tamales/hash	_____	_____	_____
3. Entrecotes	_____	_____	_____
Bordelaise	_____	_____	_____
4. Hamburgers/	_____	_____	_____
meatloaf	_____	_____	_____
5. Stuffed flank steak	_____	_____	_____
6. New England	_____	_____	_____
boiled dinner	_____	_____	_____
7. Tournedos Rossini	_____	_____	_____
	_____	_____	_____
8. London broil	_____	_____	_____
9. Beef Wellington	_____	_____	_____
	_____	_____	_____
10. Roast beef	_____	_____	_____
11. Beef roulade	_____	_____	_____
12. Beef fajitas	_____	_____	_____
13. Beef stew	_____	_____	_____
14. Chili con carne	_____	_____	_____
	_____	_____	_____
15. Minute steak	_____	_____	_____
	_____	_____	_____

13E. Multiple Choice

For each question below, choose the one response that correctly answers the question.

1. The outside round and the eye of the round together are called the:
   a. top round
   b. bottom round
   c. steamship round
   d. primal round

2. A carcass of beef weighs:
   a. between 600 and 950 pounds
   b. up to 1,000 pounds
   c. from 500 to more than 800 pounds
   d. between 400 and 600 pounds

3. The three fabricated cuts from the tenderloin are:
   a. porterhouse steak, tournedos, and chateaubriand
   b. butt tenderloin, filet mignon, and tournedos
   c. chateaubriand, short loin, and loin eye
   d. tournedos, chateaubriand, and filet mignon

4. "Butterflying" is a preparation technique which:
   a. makes the cut of meat thinner
   b. makes the meat more tender
   c. improves the flavor of the meat
   d. improves the appearance of the meat

13F. Matching I

Match each of the primal cuts in List A with the appropriate description in List B. Each choice in List B can only be used once.

List A

_____ 1. Rib

_____ 2. Chuck

_____ 3. Short Loin

_____ 4. Flank

List B

a. Produces the boneless strip loin, which can be roasted whole or cut into steaks

b. This cut is located in the hindquarter between the short loin and the round.

c. The eye of this cut is well exercised, quite tender, and contains large quantities of marbling. It is suitable for roasting.

d. The animal constantly uses the muscle in this primal cut, therefore it is tough, contains high levels of connective tissue, and is very flavorful.

e. This primal cut produces the hanging tenderloin which is very tender and can be cooked by any method.

13G. Matching II

Match the following cooking processes with the appropriate cut of meat. Each cooking process matches *only* two (2) cuts of meat.

1. Grill

2. Roast

3. Braise

a. _____ Shank
b. _____ Porterhouse
c. _____ Rib
d. _____ Top round
e. _____ Strip loin
f. _____ Short ribs

13H. Chapter Review

For each question below, circle either True or False to indicate the correct answer.

1. The hanging tenderloin is part of the flank.
   True   False

2. The meat from the chuck is less flavorful than meat from the tenderloin.
   True   False

3. A porterhouse steak is a fabricated cut from the tenderloin.
   True   False

4. Prime rib of beef refers to the quality USDA grade.
   True   False

5. The subprimal and fabricated cuts from the short loin are the most tender and expensive cuts of beef.
   True   False

6. The subprimal and fabricated cuts from the sirloin are not as tender as those from the strip loin.
   True   False

7. The short loin can be cut across to produce porterhouse, T-bone and club steaks.
   True   False

8. Pastrami is made from the meat in the short plate.
   True   False

CHAPTER 14

VEAL

TEST YOUR KNOWLEDGE

The practice sets provided below have been designed to test your comprehension of the information found in this chapter. It is recommended that you read this chapter completely before attempting these questions.

14A. Terminology

Fill in the blank spaces with the correct definition.

For each primal cut of Veal listed below, describe the following:
    a. % of carcass weight
    b. Bone structure
    c. Muscle structure
    d. Cooking processes applied

1. Veal _____

    a. _____

    b. _____

    c. _____

    d. _____

2. Shoulder _____

    a. _____

    b. _____

    c. _____

    d. _____

3. Foreshank & breast _____

    a. _____

    b. _____

    c. _____

    d. _____

4. Rib _____

    a. _____

    b. _____

    c. _____

    d. _____

5. Loin _____

    a. _____

    b. _____

    c. _____

    d. _____

6. Leg _____

    a. _____

    b. _____

    c. _____

    d. _____

7. Foresaddle _____

8. Hindsaddle _____

9. Back _____

10. Veal side _____

11. Sweetbreads _____

12. Calves' liver _____

13. Kidneys _____

14. Veal scallops _____

15. Emince _____

14B. Primal Cuts of Veal

Identify the primal cuts of veal indicated in the following diagram and write their names in the spaces provided.

1. _____

2. _____

3. _____

4. _____

5. _____

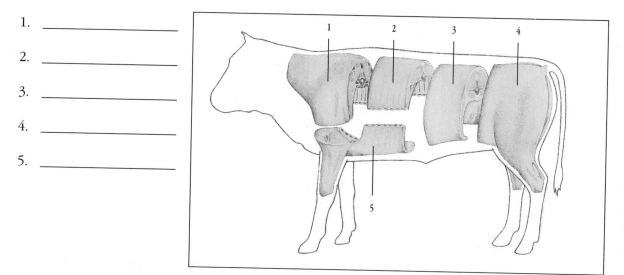

14C. Cuts of Veal and Applied Cooking Methods

Name the cooking method applied to the main ingredient in each of the following dishes. Also, identify a subprimal and a primal cut of meat from which the main ingredient is taken.

Name of Dish	Cooking Method	Subprimal/ Fabricated Cut	Primal Cut
1. Blanquette/ fricasee			
2. Veal rib eye Marchand de vin			
3. Stuffed veal breast			
4. Veal chop with mushroom sauce			
5. Blanquette			
6. Veal sweetbreads			

7. Kidney pie   _____   _____   _____

8. Veal patties   _____   _____   _____

9. Meatballs   _____   _____   _____

10. Tenderloin   _____   _____   _____

11. Veal marsala   _____   _____   _____

12. Calves liver   _____   _____   _____

13. Osso buco   _____   _____   _____

14. Veal scallopini   _____   _____   _____

15. Veal broth   _____   _____   _____

14D. Short Answer

Provide a short response that correctly answers each of the questions below.

1. Briefly describe the eight (8) basic steps to be followed when boning a leg of veal, beginning with:

    a. <u>Remove the shank</u> _____

    b. _____

    c. _____

    d. _____

    e. _____

    f. _____

    g. _____

    h. _____

2. Name the six (6) muscles in the leg of veal.

    a. _____

    b. _____

    c. _____

d. _____

e. _____

f. _____

3. Name the three (3) subprimal cuts from the rib and three (3) from the loin and provide a menu example of each cut.

Primal Cut	Subprimal/Fabricated Cut	Menu Example
a. Rib	_____	_____
b. Rib	_____	_____
c. Rib	_____	_____
a. Loin	_____	_____
b. Loin	_____	_____
c. Loin	_____	_____

4. Compare and contrast formula-fed veal with free-range veal. Discuss the advantages and disadvantages of each.

_____

_____

_____

_____

_____

_____

_____

14E. Matching I

Match the primal cuts in List A with the appropriate definitions in List B. Each choice in List B can only be used once.

List A

_____ 1. Leg
_____ 2. Shoulder

_____ 3. Foreshank
     and Breast
_____ 4. Loin

List B

a. A cut of veal similar to the chuck in beef.

b. A primal cut of veal which is located just below the shoulder and rib section in the front of the carcass.

c. The primal cut that produces the short tenderloin.

d. The bones in this cut are still soft, due to the immaturity of the animal.

_____ 5. Rib

e. The primal cut that yields the most tender meat.

f. Made up of portions of the backbone, tail bone, hip bone, aitch bone, round bone, and shank.

14F. Matching II

Match each of the following cooking processes with the appropriate cut of meat. Each process matches *only* two (2) cuts of meat.

List A

1. Saute

2. Roast

3. Braise

List B

a. _____ Split veal rack

b. _____ Calves' liver

c. _____ Veal shank

d. _____ Whole veal loin

e. _____ Veal emince

f. _____ Veal breast

14G. Chapter Review

For each question below, circle either True or False to indicate the correct answer.

1. Veal scallops are taken from large pieces of veal and are cut on the bias, across the grain of the meat.
   True   False

2. Veal flesh begins to change color when the animal consumes iron in its food.
   True   False

3. Sweetbreads are pressed to remove the impurities.
   True   False

4. Veal émincé are cut with the grain, from small pieces of meat.
   True   False

5. Veal scallops are pounded in order to make them more tender.
   True   False

6. Sweetbreads become larger as the animal ages.
   True   False

7. Veal liver has a more delicate flavor than beef liver.
   True   False

8. The hindshank and foreshank of veal are prepared and cooked in the same manner.
   True   False

CHAPTER 15

LAMB

TEST YOUR KNOWLEDGE

The practice sets provided below have been designed to test your comprehension of the information found in this chapter. It is recommended that you read the chapter completely before attempting these questions.

15A. Terminology

Fill in the blank spaces with the correct definition.

For each primal cut of Lamb listed below, describe the following:
    a.   % of carcass weight
    b.   Bone structure
    c.   Muscle structure
    d.   Cooking processes applied

1. Lamb   _____

2. Shoulder   _____

    a. _____

    b. _____

    c. _____

    d. _____

3. Breast   _____

    a. _____

    b. _____

c. _____

d. _____

4. Rack _____

   a. _____

   b. _____

   c. _____

   d. _____

5. French _____

6. Loin _____

   a. _____

   b. _____

   c. _____

   d. _____

7. Leg _____

   a. _____

   b. _____

   c. _____

   d. _____

8. Foresaddle _____

9. Hindsaddle _____

10. Back _____

11. Bracelet _____

15B. Primal Cuts of Lamb

Identify the primal cuts of lamb indicated in the following diagram and write their names in the spaces provided below.

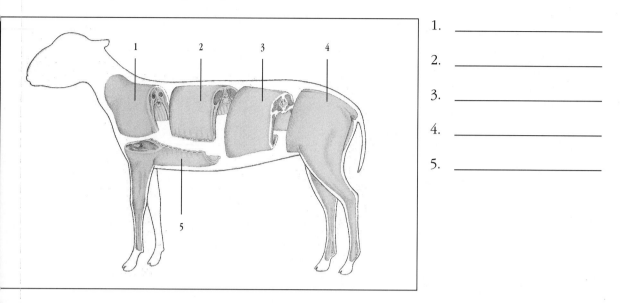

1. _____

2. _____

3. _____

4. _____

5. _____

15C. Subprimal or Fabricated Cuts

For each primal cut named above, name two subprimal cuts and an appropriate cooking method for each of these cuts.

Primal Cut	Subprimal/Fabricated Cut	Cooking Methods
1.	a. _____	_____
	b. _____	_____
2.	a. _____	_____
	b. _____	_____
3.	a. _____	_____
	b. _____	_____
4.	a. _____	_____
	b. _____	_____
5.	a. _____	_____
	b. _____	_____

15D. Cuts of Lamb and Applied Cooking Methods

Name the cooking method applied to the main ingredient in each of the following lamb dishes. Also, identify a subprimal and a primal cut of meat from which the main ingredient is taken.

Name of Dish	Cooking Method	Subprimal/ Fabricated Cut	Primal Cut
1. Lamb kebabs	_____	_____	_____
2. Lamb curry	_____	_____	_____
3. Noisettes of lamb with roasted garlic sauce	_____	_____	_____
4. Lamb stew	_____	_____	_____
5. Broiled lamb with mustard and hazelnut crust	_____	_____	_____
6. Lamb breast stuffed with mushrooms	_____	_____	_____
7. Rack of lamb	_____	_____	_____
8. Leg of lamb	_____	_____	_____

15E. Short Answer

Provide a short response that correctly answers the questions below.

1. Briefly describe the six (6) basic steps to be followed when frenching a rack of lamb.

   a. _____

   b. _____

   c. _____

   d. _____

   e. _____

   f. _____

2. Briefly describe the four (4) basic steps to be followed when trimming a leg of lamb for roasting/grilling.

   a. _____

   b. _____

   c. _____

   d. _____

3. Briefly describe the eight (8) basic steps to be followed when preparing a loin of lamb for roasting.

a. _____

b. _____

c. _____

d. _____

e. _____

f. _____

g. _____

h. _____

15F. Chapter Review

For each question below, circle either True or False to indicate the correct answer.

1. The lamb carcass is classified into two parts—the hindquarter and the forequarter.
   True   False

2. The term "spring lamb" applies to animals that are born between February and May.
   True   False

3. The primal cuts of both veal and lamb are broken down into bilateral halves.
   True   False

4. The primal leg of lamb is rarely left whole.
   True   False

5. The leg of lamb can be broken down to produce steaks.
   True   False

6. The chine bone runs through the loin of lamb.
   True   False

7. The "fell" refers to thin layer of connective tissue on the outside of the loin of lamb.
   True   False

8. Denver ribs are ribs that are cut from the breast of lamb.
   True   False

CHAPTER 16

PORK

TEST YOUR KNOWLEDGE

The practice sets provided below have been designed to test your comprehension of the information found in this chapter. It is recommended that you read the chapter completely before attempting these questions.

16A. Terminology

Fill in the blank spaces with the correct definition.

For each primal cut of Pork listed below, describe the following:
   a. % of carcass weight
   b. Bone structure
   c. Muscle structure
   d. Cooking processes applied

  1. Shoulder   _____

     a. _____

     b. _____

     c. _____

     d. _____

  2. Boston Butt   _____

     a. _____

     b. _____

     c. _____

     d. _____

3. Belly _____

    a. _____

    b. _____

    c. _____

    d. _____

4. Loin _____

    a. _____

    b. _____

    c. _____

    d. _____

5. Fresh ham _____

    a. _____

    b. _____

    c. _____

    d. _____

16B. Primal Cuts of Pork

Identify the primal cuts of pork indicated in the following diagram and write their names in the spaces provided below.

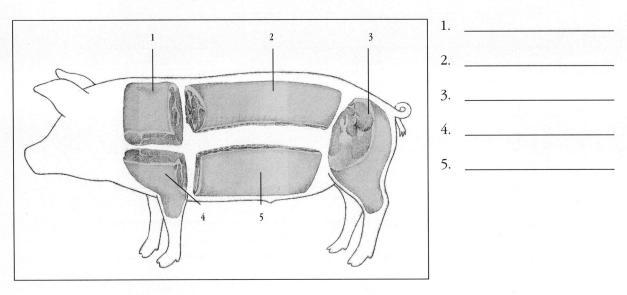

1. _____

2. _____

3. _____

4. _____

5. _____

16C. Subprimal or Fabricated Cuts

For each primal cut named above, name a subprimal cut and an appropriate cooking method. Indicate in the appropriate columns(s) whether these cuts are usually smoked or fresh (or both).

Primal Cut	Subprimal/ Fabricated Cut	Cooking Methods	Cured & Smoked	Fresh
1.	_____	_____	_____	_____
2.	_____	_____	_____	_____
3.	_____	_____	_____	_____
4.	_____	_____	_____	_____
5.	_____	_____	_____	_____

Example:

Fresh ham	Hock	Braise	X

16D. Cuts of Pork and Applied Cooking Methods

Name the cooking method applied to the main ingredient in each of the following recipes. Also identify a subprimal and a primal cut of meat from which the main ingredient is taken.

Name of Dish	Cooking Method	Subprimal/ Fabricated Cut	Primal Cut
1. Roast pork with apricots & almonds	_____	_____	_____
2. Choucroute	_____	_____	_____
3. Pork tenderloin	_____	_____	_____
4. Pork chops	_____	_____	_____
5. Spare ribs	_____	_____	_____
6. Smoked picnic shoulder	_____	_____	_____
7. Breakfast meat	_____	_____	_____

16E. Short Answer

Provide a short response that correctly answers the questions below.

1. Briefly describe the three (3) basic steps to be followed when boning a pork loin.

    a. _____

    b. _____

    c. _____

2. Name six (6) fabricated cuts that are most often smoked and cured.

a. _____

b. _____

c. _____

d. _____

e. _____

f. _____

16F. Matching

Match the primal cuts in List A with the appropriate definitions in List B. Each choice in List B can only be used once.

List A

_____ 1. Boston butt

_____ 2. Shoulder

_____ 3. Belly

_____ 4. Loin

_____ 5. Fresh ham

List B

a. A primal cut that is very fatty with strips of lean meat.

b. The primal cut from which the most tender portion of pork is taken.

c. A primal cut which contains large muscles and relatively small amounts of connective tissue. It may be smoked and cured or cooked fresh.

d. A primal cut with a good percentage of fat to lean meat—ideal when a solid piece of pork is required for a recipe.

e. A single, very tender eye muscle that can be braised/roasted/sautéed.

f. One of the toughest cuts of pork. It has a relatively high ratio of bone to lean meat, is relatively inexpensive and widely available.

16G. Chapter Review

For each question below, circle either True or False to indicate the correct answer.

1. The Boston butt is located in the hindquarter.
   True   False

2. Pork is unique because the ribs and loin are considered one primal cut.
   True   False

3. The term "meat packing" originated in colonial times when pork was packed into barrels for shipment abroad.
   True   False

4. The foreshank is also known as the ham hock.
   True   False

5. Center-cut pork chops are chops that are split open to form a pocket.
   True   False

6. The belly is used to make Canadian bacon.
   True   False

7. Backfat is the layer of fat between the skin and the lean muscle of the pork loin.
   True   False

8. The two primal cuts that produce ribs are the loin and the belly.
   True   False

9. Hogs are bred to produce short loins.
   True   False

10. Picnic ham is made from the hog's hind leg.
    True   False

*P*OULTRY

*T*EST *Y*OUR *K*NOWLEDGE

The practice sets provided below have been designed to test your comprehension of the information found in this chapter. It is recommended that you read the chapter completely before attempting these questions.

17A. Terminology

Fill in the blank spaces with the correct definition.

1. Duckling   _____

2. Guinea   _____

3. Squab   _____

4. Dinde   _____

5. Ratites   _____

6. Giblets   _____

7. Foie gras   _____

8. Supreme   _____

9. A point   _____

10. Trussing   _____

11. Barding _____

12. Basting _____

13. Dressing _____

17B. Short Answer

Provide a short response that correctly answers each of the questions below.

1. List five (5) important guidelines for stuffing poultry.

   a. _____

   b. _____

   c. _____

   d. _____

   e. _____

2. Name one similarity and one major difference between poultry and red meats.

   Similarity: _____

   _____

   Difference: _____

   _____

3. Poultry is a highly perishable product and improper storage can lead to food poisoning. Discuss the guidelines for storing poultry products under the following headings.
   *Include *exact* temperatures and times in this answer.

   Storage under refrigeration: _____

   _____

   Freezing: _____

   _____

   Thawing: _____

   _____

   Reheating: _____

4. List five (5) differences between the rearing and sale of free-range chicken compared to traditionally reared chicken.

a. _____

b. _____

c. _____

d. _____

e. _____

5. What are the six (6) kinds of poultry?

a. _____

b. _____

c. _____

d. _____

e. _____

f. _____

6. For each of the following cooking methods, give a recipe example and accompaniment for the poultry item.

Cooking Method	Recipe Example	Accompaniment
Sauté	_____	_____
Pan-fry	_____	_____
Simmer/Poach	_____	_____
Braise/Stew	_____	_____

7. Describe five (5) ways to prevent cross-contamination when handling poultry.

a. _____

b. _____

c. _____

d. _____

e. _____

8. Describe the six (6) steps for portioning poultry into 8 pieces.

a. _____

b. _____

c. _____

d. _____

e. _____

f. _____

17C. Matching

Match each of the terms in List A with the appropriate letter definition in List B. Each choice in List B can only be used once.

List A	List B
_____ 1. Hen/stewing	a. Young tender meat, smooth skin, breastbone less flexible than a broiler's (3-5 months).
_____ 2. Broiler/fryer	b. Mature female, less tender meat, nonflexible breastbone (over 10 months).
_____ 3. Roaster	c. Young immature offspring of Cornish chicken, very flavorful (5-6 weeks).
_____ 4. Capon	d. Rich, tender dark meat with large amounts of fat, soft windpipe (6 months or less).
_____ 5. Game hen	e. Young with soft, smooth skin, lean with flexible breastbone (13 weeks).
	f. Surgically castrated male, tender meat, smooth skin, high proportion of light to dark meat, relatively high fat content (under 8 months).

17D. Fill in the Blank

Fill in the blank provided with the response that correctly completes the statement.

1. The color difference between the legs and wings of chicken and turkey is due to a higher concentration of the _____ called _____ in the tissue.

2. The internal temperature of fully cooked poultry should be between _____ and _____.

3. The most commonly used duck in foodservice operations is a _____. Its meat is different from chicken in two ways: the flesh is _____ and has large amounts of _____.

4. Chicken is often marinated in a mixture of _____.

   A common example of a chicken marinade is _____ sauce.

17E. Multiple Choice

For each question below, choose one response that correctly answers the question.

1. Poultry should be refrigerated between:
   a. 30–35° F
   b. 33–36° F
   c. 32–34° F
   d. 30–38° F

2. Which of the following groups does not fall into the "poultry" category?
   a. chicken, duck, pigeon
   b. duck, pheasant, goose
   c. pigeon, guineas, chicken
   d. none of the above

3. The poultry that is sold in wholesale or retail outlets carries the USDA Grade
   a. A
   b. C
   c. B
   d. all of the above

17F. Chapter Review

For each question below, circle either True or False to indicate the correct answer.

1. Poultry fat has a higher melting point than other animal fats.
   True   False

2. Duck and goose must be roasted at a higher temperature in order to render as much fat from the skin as possible.
   True   False

3. Myoglobin is a protein that stores oxygen.
   True   False

4. The longer chicken is left in a marinade, the better the flavor.
   True   False

5. Dark meat takes less time to cook than light meat.
   True   False

6. Poultry should not be frozen below -18° C/0° F.
   True   False

7. The skin color of poultry is partly affected by the amount of sunlight to which it is exposed.
   True   False

8. Quality USDA grades do not reflect the tenderness of poultry.
   True   False

9. Older male birds have more flavor than female birds.
   True   False

10. When foie gras is overcooked it becomes tough.
    True   False

11. A young pigeon is called a yearling.
    True   False

12. The gizzard is a term used to describe the chicken's neck.
    True   False

13. A capon is a type of pigeon.
    True   False

14. Poultry are divided into classes based on the sex of the bird.
    True   False

15. Most ratite meat is cut from the back of birds slaughtered between 10 to 13 months.
    True   False

16. Ostrich meat is best cooked well done.
    True   False

17. Poultry should not be marinated for longer than two hours.
    True   False

18. After marinating poultry, the marinade may be stored for future use.
    True   False

19. Poultry should be cooked to an internal temperature of 160° F to 170° F.
    True   False

20. Fresh chicken should be stored refrigerated between 32° F and 34° F for up to four days.
    True   False

CHAPTER 18

GAME

TEST YOUR KNOWLEDGE

The practice sets provided below have been designed to test your comprehension of the information found in this chapter. It is recommended that you read the chapter completely before attempting these questions.

18A. Terminology

Fill in the blank spaces with the correct definition.

For each of the following Game Animals listed below, list the following:
- a. Source of animal
- b. Composition of flesh
- c. Recommended cooking methods

1. Antelope _____

    a. _____

    b. _____

    c. _____

2. Bison _____

    a. _____

    b. _____

    c. _____

3. Venison _____

    a. _____

    b. _____

    c. _____

4. Rabbit _____

    a. _____

    b. _____

    c. _____

5. Wild Boar _____

    a. _____

    b. _____

    c. _____

6. Partridge _____

    a. _____

    b. _____

    c. _____

7. Pheasant _____

    a. _____

    b. _____

    c. _____

8. Quail _____

    a. _____

    b. _____

    c. _____

9. Frogs _____

10. Hanging Game _____

18B. Short Answer

Provide a short response that correctly answers the questions below.

1. List three (3) uses for tougher cuts of game.

    a. _____

    b. _____

    c. _____

2. Explain the process and purpose for hanging wild game.

Process: _____

_____

_____

_____

Purpose: _____

_____

3. Describe the origins and makeup of Beefalo.

_____

_____

_____

_____

4. Describe the guidelines for refrigeration and freezing of game.

_____

_____

_____

_____

18C. Multiple Choice

For each question below, choose the one response that correctly answers the question.

1. Which of the following cannot be categorized as furred game?
   a. antelope
   b. pheasant
   c. bison
   d. rabbit

2. Due to the lean nature of game birds, they are barded and cooked:
   a. medium
   b. rare
   c. medium rare
   d. well done

3. Which one of the following is *not* a member of the deer family?
   a. elk
   b. bison
   c. mule deer
   d. moose

4. Feathered game include:
   a. pheasant, quail, woodcock
   b. partridge, pheasant, pigeon
   c. turkey, lark, squab
   d. guinea, goose, duck

5. Quail weighs approximately:
   a. 10–12 ounces
   b. 1–2 pounds
   c. 4–5 pounds
   d. none of the above

6. The most popular game bird is:
   a. quail
   b. partridge
   c. pheasant
   d. woodcock

18D. Chapter Review

For each question below, circle either True or False to indicate the correct answer.

1. Most farmed deer is not slaughtered or processed in the slaughterhouse.
   True   False

2. Wild antelope, venison, and rabbit are not subject to inspection under federal law.
   True   False

3. A mature boar (3-4 years old) has a better flavor than a younger animal.
   True   False

4. Wild game birds can be purchased by request from most butchers.
   True   False

5. Wild boar is closely related to the domestic pig.
   True   False

6. Game is higher in fat and vitamins than most other meats.
   True   False

7. Venison is very moist due the marbling through the tissue.
   True   False

8. Large game animals are usually sold in primal portions.
   True   False

9. Furred game meat has a finer grain than other meats.
   True   False

10. The aroma, texture, and flavor of game is affected by the lifestyle of the animal.
    True   False

11. Antelope, deer and rabbit are the game most widely available to foodservice operations.
    True   False

12. The flesh of game is generally moist and tender.
    True   False

13. During the hanging process, carbohydrates convert into lactic acid, which tenderizes the flesh.
    True   False

14. Commercially raised game should *always* be marinated.
    True   False

Fish and Shellfish

Test Your Knowledge

The practice sets provided below have been designed to test your comprehension of the information found in this chapter. It is recommended that you read the chapter completely before attempting these questions.

19A. Terminology

Fill in the blank spaces with the correct definition.

1. En papillotte   _____

2. Cephalopods   _____

3. Mollusks   _____

4. Anadromous   _____

5. Aquafarmed   _____

6. Bivalves   _____

7. Pan dressed   _____

8. Univalves   _____

9. Round fish   _____

10. Whole or round   _____

11. Crustaceans   _____

12. Butterflied   _____

13. Steak _____

14. Submersion poaching _____

15. Drawn _____

16. Cuisson _____

17. Fillet _____

18. Shallow poaching _____

19. Tranche _____

20. Flat fish _____

21. Wheel or center cut _____

19B. Multiple Choice

For each question below, choose the one response that correctly answers the question.

1. To maintain optimum freshness, fish and shellfish should be stored at what temperature?
   a. 40° F.
   b. 30–34° F.
   c. 40–45° F.
   d. 38–40° F.

2. Fish are graded:
   a. USDA Prime, Choice, Select, or Utility
   b. Type 1, Type 2, Type 3
   c. Premium, Commercial Grade, Cutter/Canner
   d. USDC A, B, or C

3. Clams, mussels, and oysters should be stored:
   a. at 36° F.
   b. on ice and in refrigeration.
   c. in boxes or net bags.
   d. at 20 % humidity.

4. Univalves and bivalves are both examples of:
   a. mollusks
   b. cephalopods
   c. clams
   d. crustaceans

5. The "universal" meaning of *prawn* refers to a:
   a. shrimp sautéd in garlic and butter
   b. all shrimp, freshwater or marine variety
   c. shrimp from the Gulf of Mexico
   d. freshwater variety of shrimp only

6. In terms of the market forms of fish, *dressed* refers to:
   a. viscera removed
   b. viscera, gills, fins, and scales removed
   c. as caught, intact
   d. viscera, fins, and gills removed, scaled, and tail trimmed

7. The most important commercial variety of salmon is:
   a. Atlantic
   b. Pacific
   c. Chinook
   d. King

8. Which type of sole cannot be caught off the coastline of the United States?
   a. Lemon
   b. English
   c. Petrale
   d. Dover

9. Mackerel, wahoo, herring, sardines, and salmon have similar characteristics in that:
   a. the color of their flesh is the same
   b. they all migrate
   c. their flesh is moderate-highly oily
   d. their geographic availability is the same

10. All clams are examples of:
    a. cephalopods
    b. crustaceans
    c. univalves
    d. bivalves

11. The best-selling fish in America is:
    a. Atlantic salmon
    b. lemon sole
    c. cod
    d. ahi tuna

12. When cooking fish fillets with the skin on, what can be done to prevent the fillet from curling?
    a. Cook fillet at a high temperature, short time
    b. Cook fillet at a low temperature, longer time
    c. Score the skin of the fish before cooking
    d. Flatten the fillet by weighing down with a semi-heavy object during cooking

19C. Market Forms of Fish

Identify the market forms indicated in the following diagram and write their names in the spaces provided below.

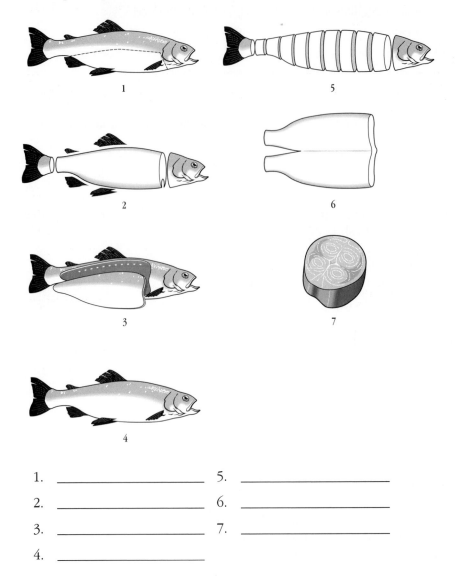

1. _____ 5. _____

2. _____ 6. _____

3. _____ 7. _____

4. _____

19D. Short Answer

Provide a short response that correctly answers each of the questions below.

1. Give two (2) reasons why fish fillets and steaks are the best market forms to bake.

   a. _____

   b. _____

2. List the four (4) guidelines for determining the doneness of fish and shellfish.

   a. _____

   b. _____

   c. _____

   d. _____

3. List four (4) cooking methods that would be appropriate for preparing a tranche of salmon.

   a. _____

   b. _____

   c. _____

   d. _____

4. List two (2) oily and two (2) lean fish that grill well.

   oily   *lean*

   a. _____   c. _____

   b. _____   d. _____

5. Name four (4) types of shellfish good for sautéing.

   a. _____   c. _____

   b. _____   d. _____

6. List three (3) dishes that exemplify why shellfish are good for baking.

   a. _____

   b. _____

   c. _____

7. Explain two (2) reasons why combination cooking methods are not traditionally used to prepare fish and shellfish.

   a. _____

   b. _____

8. List four (4) of the seven (7) quality points used to determine the freshness of fish.

a. _____   c. _____

b. _____   d. _____

19E. Chapter Review

For each question below circle either True or False to indicate the correct answer.

1. All fish are eligible for grading.
   True   False

2. Fish and shellfish inspections are mandatory.
   True   False

3. A lobster is an example of a crustacean.
   True   False

4. Fatty fish are especially good for baking.
   True   False

5. The only difference between Maine lobsters and spiny lobsters is the geographic location where they're caught.
   True   False

6. Atlantic hard-shell clams are also known as geoducks.
   True   False

7. Fillet of halibut is a good fish to pan-fry.
   True   False

8. Cooking fish or shellfish en papillote is an example of baking.
   True   False

9. Shellfish has as much cholesterol as lamb.
   True   False

10. Salmon gets its pink-red flesh color from the crustaceans it eats.
    True   False

11. Halibut and sole are examples of flat fish.
    True   False

12. The best market form to purchase monk fish in is steaks.
    True   False

13. Surimi has equal nutritional value to the real fish and shellfish it replaces.
    True   False

14. Crustaceans are shellfish.
    True   False

15. The FDA permits the practice of marketing many types of flounder as sole.
    True   False

Eggs

TEST YOUR KNOWLEDGE

The practice sets provided below have been designed to test your comprehension of the information found in this chapter. It is recommended that you read the chapter completely before attempting these questions.

20A. Terminology

Fill in the blank spaces with the correct definition.

1. Soft boiled   _____

2. Chalazae chords   _____

3. Shell   _____

4. Pasteurization   _____

5. Sunny-side up   _____

6. Yolk   _____

7. Hard boiled   _____

8. Egg White   _____

9. Over easy   _____

10. Basted eggs   _____

11. Over hard   _____

12. Over medium   _____

20B. Multiple Choice

For each question below, choose the one response that correctly answers the question.

1. At what temperature does an egg yolk solidify (coagulate) when cooking?
   a. 135° F.-143° F.
   b. 120° F.-132° F.
   c. 160° F.-171° F.
   d. 149° F.-158° F.

2. What would be a good use for grade B eggs?
   a. as a compound in facial creams and other cosmetic products
   b. for baking, scrambling, or the production of bulk egg products
   c. grade B eggs are not recommended for use in foodservice operations
   d. for frying, poaching, or cooking in the shell

3. What should a chef do to help the egg whites cling together when poaching an egg?
   a. Add salt to the water
   b. Add a small amount of white vinegar or other acid to the water
   c. Add the egg to the cooking liquid before it has a chance to simmer
   d. Use only Grade A eggs

4. In-shell cooking of eggs uses what method of cookery?
   a. frying
   b. steaming
   c. boiling
   d. simmering

5. Which *four* of the following are criteria for grading eggs?
   a. certification of farmer
   b. albumen
   c. spread
   d. shell
   e. breed of bird
   f. yolk

6. What is the maximum amount of time an egg dish can be left at room temperature (including preparation and service time) before it becomes potentially hazardous to consume?
   a. 20 minutes
   b. 40 minutes
   c. 1 hour
   d. 2 hours or more

7. Shirred eggs and quiche are both prepared by using a dry-heat cooking method. Which method do they have in common?
   a. Baking
   b. Roasting
   c. Frying
   d. Sauteing

8. Egg yolks do not contain as much cholesterol as once feared. According to the American Heart Association, how many eggs per week can be consumed and still maintain a balanced diet?
   a. Up to two
   b. Up to four
   c. Up to six
   d. Up to ten

9. Which one of the following statements is *false* about the definition of a frittata? Frittatas are:
   a. omelets containing a generous amount of ingredients that are folded in half when served.
   b. of Spanish-Italian origin
   c. started on the stovetop, then place in the oven, or under a salamander or broiler to finish cooking
   d. different sizes, depending on the size pan used to prepare them.

10. Cartons of fresh, uncooked (refrigerated) eggs in the shell are safe to use in cooking:
   a. until the expiration date stamped on the package.
   b. until three weeks beyond the packing date stamped on the package.
   c. until four to five weeks beyond the packing date stamped on the package.
   d. up to three months after they are laid by the chicken.

20C. Identification

In reference to the diagram below, label the parts of the egg indicated.

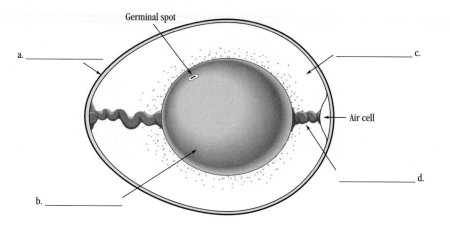

20D. Chapter Review

For each question below, circle either True or False to indicate the correct answer.

1. Egg whites solidify (coagulate) when cooked at temperatures between 144° F. and 149° F.

   True   False

2. Shell color has an effect on the grade of the egg, but not on flavor or nutrition.
   True   False

3. A French-style omelet is prepared by filling the egg mixture with a warm, savory combination of ingredients while the eggs cook in the pan.
   True   False

4. Eggs are a potentially hazardous food.
   True   False

5. To ensure maximum volume when preparing whipped egg whites, the whites should be thoroughly chilled prior to whipping.
   True   False

6. Eggs should be stored at temperatures below 35° F. and at a relative humidity of 70- 80%.
   True   False

7. Egg substitutes can replace whole eggs in all cooking applications.
   True   False

8. Egg whites contain cholesterol.
   True   False

9. When making an egg-white omelet, one should use the same amount of heat and cooking temperature as used when making a traditional omelet.
   True   False

10. Eggs used for pan-frying should be a high grade and very fresh since the yolk holds its shape better and the white spreads less.
   True   False

CHAPTER 21

DEEP-FRYING

TEST YOUR KNOWLEDGE

The practice sets provided below have been designed to test your comprehension of the information found in this chapter. It is recommended that you read this chapter completely before attempting these questions.

21A. Terminology

Fill in the blank space with the correct definition.

1. Recovery time _____

2. Swimming method _____

3. Smoke point _____

4. Basket method _____

5. Standard breading procedure _____

6. Double basket method _____

21B. Short Answer

Provide a short response that correctly answers each of the questions below.

1. What are the two (2) main components in a fritter?

    a. _____

    b. _____

2. What is the procedure for battering foods?

    a. _____

    b. _____

3. List, in proper sequence, the five (5) steps for the standard breading procedure.

a. _____

b. _____

c. _____

d. _____

e. _____

4. How can one keep his/her hands from becoming coated with breading during the standard breading procedure?

_____

5. Identify the elements that damage fryer fat and explain their effects on the fat.

Element   *Effects*

a. _____   _____

b. _____   _____

c. _____   _____

d. _____   _____

e. _____   _____

6. List two (2) reasons why most fried foods are breaded or battered.

a. _____

b. _____

7. The temperature of the fat is critical during frying. List two (2) reasons to support this statement.

a. _____

b. _____

8. List three (3) ways to determine the doneness of a fried product.

a. _____

b. _____

c. _____

9. List three (3) considerations when choosing fat for frying.

   a. _____

   b. _____

   c. _____

10. Suggest three (3) methods of holding fried products before service.

   a. _____

   b. _____

   c. _____

21C. Chapter Review

For each question below circle either True or False to indicate the correct answer.

1. The internal temperature of fried chicken should be 160–170° F.
   True   False

2. The swimming method is best to use when large quantities of foods need frying.
   True   False

3. Fryolators should be purchased according to the size of the heating unit.
   True   False

4. When making fritters, the main ingredient can be raw when put into the batter, since it will cook during the frying process.
   True   False

5. Delicately flavored foods should be fried separately from foods with strong flavors.
   True   False

6. Foods that are fried together can be a variety of sizes, as long as they brown evenly.
   True   False

7. Frying is a cooking application that utilizes dry heat.
   True   False

8. Foods should be fried between the temperatures of 325° and 375° F.
   True   False

9. Vegetable oils are the most common type of fat used for deep-frying.
   True   False

10. The primary purpose for beer in a batter is flavor.
    True   False

11. Fats used for deep fat frying are often hydrogenated to help prevent oxidation and chemical breakdown.
    True   False

12. Wire frying baskets should be filled with foods to be fried while hanging over the fat, as to prevent the possibility of dripping fat or water on the floor or work surfaces.
    True   False

13. Seasoning fried foods immediately after they are removed from the fryer will help the seasonings cling to the product better.
    True   False

14. Only tender foods should be deep fried.
    True   False

15. Frying in a saucepan on the stove top is a realistic option if a foodservice operation cannot afford a fryolator.
    True   False

16. Vegetable oils specially formulated for frying are usually composed of anti-foaming agents, preservatives, and antioxidants.
    True   False

VEGETABLES

TEST YOUR KNOWLEDGE

The practice sets provided below have been designed to test your comprehension of the information found in this chapter. It is recommended that you read the chapter completely before attempting these questions.

22A. Terminology

Fill in the blank spaces with the correct definition.

1. Parboiling _____

2. Vegetable _____

3. Beurre Noisette _____

4. Cellulose _____

5. Blanching _____

6. Refreshing or shocking _____

22B. Multiple Choice

For each question below, choose the one response that correctly answers the question.

1. A braised vegetable dish differs from a stewed vegetable dish in that it:
   a. contains an acid product
   b. is usually prepared with only one vegetable
   c. has a longer cooking time
   d. is served with a reduction of the cooking liquid

2. Grades for all vegetables include:
   a. U.S. No. 1, U.S. No. 2, U.S. No. 3
   b. U.S. Grade A, U.S. Grade B, U.S. Grade C
   c. U.S. Extra Fancy, U.S. Fancy, U.S. Extra No. 1, U.S. No. 1
   d. U.S.D.A. Recommended, U.S.D.A. Approved

3. Vegetables are considered savory because:
   a. they are an herbaceous plant that can be partially or wholly eaten
   b. they have less sugar than fruit
   c. they have little or no woody tissue
   d. they are usually eaten cooked, not raw

4. Which of the following is *false* about sautéing vegetables?
   a. The finished product should be firm to the bite, brightly colored, and show little moisture loss.
   b. All preparation of ingredients should be done in advance because the cooking process proceeds rapidly.
   c. Seasonings should be added to the pan when warming the oil or fat so their flavors have time to develop during this quick cooking process.
   d. A wide variety of vegetables can be sautéed.

5. Which one of the following is a *disadvantage* of grilling vegetables?
   a. The high heat of the cooking process kills much of the nutritional content.
   b. The types of vegetable to be grilled must be carefully selected based on their cooking times.
   c. Vegetables often need to be brushed or marinated with a little oil or fat before cooking.
   d. Smaller vegetables should be skewered to make handling easier.

6. Which of the following vegetables is *not* suitable for roasting or baking:
   a. eggplant
   b. potatoes
   c. spinach
   d. peppers

7. Fresh vegetables are sold by:
   a. case or flats
   b. degree of processing
   c. weight or count
   d. specifications

8. To preserve as many nutrients, color, and texture as possible:
   a. cut the vegetables into uniform shapes before cooking
   b. cook vegetables whole, then peel and cut
   c. add acid to the cooking liquid
   d. cook the vegetables as little as possible

9. When pan-steaming vegetables:
   a. overcooking is less likely to happen
   b. cover the cooking apparatus to retain heat
   c. more nutrients are lost than in other techniques
   d. choose only vegetables with a firm texture

10. Which of the following is true about microwave cooking?
    a. It substitutes well for all cooking techniques except broiling and grilling.
    b. It is best used as a substitute for traditional steaming.
    c. It is dangerous to use in large-scale food service operations.
    d. Its cooking process, agitating water molecules within food, depletes nutrients.

22C. Product Identification

Match each vegetable in List A with the appropriate letter in List B. Each choice in List B can only be used once.

List A	*List B*
_____ 1. Artichokes	a. A winter squash variety, especially popular in October.
_____ 2. Swiss chard	b. A type of beet only used for its greens.
_____ 3. Okra	c. A firm, orange taproot that is eaten raw or cooked.
_____ 4. Bok choy	d. Tubers that grow near oak or beech tree roots.
_____ 5. Pumpkin	e. A member of the *capsicum* family commonly used in Asian, Indian, Mexican and Latin American cuisines.
_____ 6. Tomatillos	f. From Arab and African cuisines, a pod often used for thickening.
_____ 7. Leeks	g. A sweet, onion-flavored vegetable with flat, wide leaves.
_____ 8. Truffles	h. A white-stemmed variety of southern Chinese cabbage.
_____ 9. Corn	i. Immature flowers of a thistle plant often canned or marinated.
_____ 10. Cucumbers	j. Husk tomatoes with a crisp, tart flesh.
_____ 11. Carrots	k. The immature stalks of bulb onions.
_____ 12. Hot peppers	l. A squash that comes in two varieties: pickling and slicing.
_____ 13. Bean curd	m. A plant seed that is really a grain or type of grass; grows on a cob.
	n. A cheese-like soybean product with high nutritional value, low cost, and high flavor adaptability.

22D. Chapter Review

For each question below, circle either True or False to indicate the correct answer.

1. Although frozen vegetables are often colorful, their texture may be softer than fresh vegetables.
   True   False

2. Pureed vegetables are usually prepared by first sautéing, steaming, or boiling.
   True   False

3. Winter squash is commonly braised or stewed due to its dense texture.
   True   False

4. Food is irradiated by exposing it to gamma rays to sterilize, slow ripening, or prevent sprouting.
   True   False

5. Eggplants, peppers, and tomatoes are considered "fruit-vegetables."
   True   False

6. The excess liquid used to can vegetables is what causes the contents of the can to lose nutrients and the texture to soften.
   True   False

7. Examples of legumes are dried beans and peas.
   True   False

8. The grading of vegetables is not required by the U.S.D.A.
   True   False

9. Potatoes, onions, shallots, and garlic are best stored between 34° and 40° F.
   True   False

10. An acid added to the cooking liquid causes a vegetable to resist softening and therefore require a longer cooking time.
    True   False

11. Flavenoids are found mainly in beets, cauliflower, and winter squash.
    True   False

12. Timing a vegetable as it cooks is the best way to determine doneness.
    True   False

13. The ripening of vegetables proceeds more rapidly in the presence of carbon dioxide gas.
    True   False

14. If the *only* goal is to help vegetables retain color when cooked, then an alkali is a good ingredient to add to the cooking liquid.
    True   False

15. The FDA classifies food irradiation as a preservative.
    True   False

CHAPTER 23

POTATOES, GRAINS, AND PASTA

TEST YOUR KNOWLEDGE

The practice sets provided below have been designed to test your comprehension of the information found in this chapter. It is recommended that you read the chapter completely before attempting these questions.

23A. Terminology

Fill in the blank spaces with the correct definition.

1. Extruded _____

2. Sfoglia _____

3. Tossing method _____

4. Converted rice _____

5. New potatoes _____

6. Dumpling _____

7. Hulling _____

8. Medium-grain rice _____

9. Endosperm _____

10. Filled dumpling _____

11. Berry _____

12. Durum wheat _____

13. Mealy potatoes _____

14. Plain/drop dumpling _____

15. Germ _____

16. Still-frying method _____

17. Groat _____

18. Waxy potatoes _____

19. Hull _____

20. Short-grain rice _____

21. Instant/quick cooking rice_____

22. Cracking _____

23. Brown rice _____

24. Masa harina _____

25. Pearling _____

26. White rice _____

27. Long-grain rice _____

28. Grinding _____

29. Bran _____

23B. Short Answer

Provide a short response that correctly answers each of the questions below.

1. Why is it so important to use ample water when cooking pasta?

   _____

2. Why shouldn't a baked potato be cooked by wrapping in foil or microwaving?

   a. _____

   b. _____

3. Name three (3) dishes that are traditionally made with short-grained rice.

   a. _____

   b. _____

   c. _____

4. The finest commercial pastas are made with pure semolina flour. Why?

   _____

5. Duchesse potatoes are considered the mother to many classical potato dishes. List four (4) different classical dishes prepared from Duchesse, briefly describing the ingredients.

   a. _____

   b. _____

   c. _____

   d. _____

6. Identify the three (3) main shapes of Italian pasta.

   a. _____   c. _____

   b. _____

7. What are the three (3) basic cooking methods for cooking grains?

   a. _____   c. _____

   b. _____

8. Give three (3) reasons for soaking most dried Asian noodles in hot water before cooking.

   a. _____

   b. _____

   c. _____

23C. Multiple Choice

For each question below, choose the one response that correctly answers each question.

1. What is the difference between cooking fresh pasta and dry, factory-produced pasta?
   a. Fresh pasta takes significantly less time to cook
   b. Dried pasta should be cooked to order
   c. Dried pasta takes significantly less time to cook
   d. Fresh pasta contains a much different list of ingredients

2. Which of the following grains *cannot* be used to make risotto?
   a. Barley
   b. Oats
   c. Buckwheat
   d. Arborio rice

3. American-grown rice does not need to be rinsed before cooking because:
   a. all of the starch will be washed away
   b. the rice will become soggy before cooking
   c. rinsing will result in a sticky rice
   d. such rice is generally clean and free of insects

4. When boiling pasta, "ample water" is defined by measurements:
   a. 1 quart of water to 1 pound of pasta
   b. 2 quarts of water to 1 pound of pasta
   c. 15:1 ratio of water to pasta
   d. 1 gallon of water to 1 pound of pasta

5. Which of the following is *false* about converted rice? It:
   a. tastes the same as regular milled white rice.
   b. retains more nutrients than regular milled white rice.
   c. has been pearled in order to remove the surface starch.
   d. cooks more slowly than regular milled white rice.

6. Why is long grained rice more versatile and popular than other rices? Long grained rice:
   a. has a higher nutritional content than short or medium grained rice
   b. remains firm and separate when cooked properly
   c. is far more affordable for a larger variety of foodservice operations
   d. is easier and faster to cook than the other rices

7. Which type of potato would be good for making Potatoes Berny?
   a. Mealy potatoes
   b. Waxy potatoes
   c. New potatoes
   d. Sweet potatoes

8. Which statement is *false* about the nutritional content of grains?
   a. They contain all of the essential amino acids
   b. They are high in fat
   c. They are a good source of dietary fiber
   d. They are a good source for vitamins and minerals

9. Which of the following flours is used to make Asian noodles?
   a. Potato
   b. Bean
   c. Corn
   d. Oat

23D. Chapter Review

For each question below, circle either True or False to indicate the correct answer.

1. Grains cooked by the risotto or pilaf method are first coated with hot fat.
   True   False

2. Medium-grain rice is best served fresh and piping hot.
   True   False

3. The only grain eaten fresh as a vegetable is corn.
   True   False

4. Making a dough with semolina flour makes it softer, more supple, and easier to work with.
   True   False

5. Asian noodle dough can be used to make dumplings.
   True   False

6. "Yam" is an industry term for sweet potato.
   True   False

7. Potatoes should be stored between 40° and 50° F.
   True   False

8. The best applications for mealy potatoes are sautéing and pan-frying.
   True   False

9. A ravioli is a dumpling.
   True   False

10. Fresh pasta is best when cooked to order.
    True   False

11. Top quality Russet potatoes are recommended for deep-frying.
    True   False

12. Three basic cooking methods are used to prepare grains: simmering, risotto and pilaf.
    True   False

13. The standard ratio for cooking rice is 1 part liquid to 1 part rice.
    True   False

14. Pasta is widely used in the cuisines of Asia, North America and Europe.
    True   False

15. Generally, cracked wheat and bulgur can be substituted for one another in recipes.
    True   False

16. Buckwheat is neither a wheat nor a grain.
    True   False

CHAPTER 24

Salads and Salad Dressing

Test Your Knowledge

The practice sets provided below have been designed to test your comprehension of the information found in this chapter. It is recommended that you read the chapter completely before attempting these questions.

24A. Terminology

Fill in the blank spaces with the correct definition.

1. Dressing _____

2. Bound salads _____

3. Mesclun _____

4. Base _____

5. Basic French dressing _____

6. Vegetable salads _____

7. Emulsified sauce _____

8. Green salads _____

9. Garnish _____

10. Composed salad _____

11. Body _____

12. Tossed salad _____

13. Fruit salad _____

24B. Multiple Choice

For each question below, choose the one response that correctly answers the question.

1. What is the best type of oil to use when making mayonnaise?
   a. Nut oils
   b. Vegetable oils
   c. Seed oils
   d. Olive oils

2. What are the *two* forms in which lettuce grow?
   a. Bunch and leaf
   b. Leaf and head
   c. Head and stalks
   d. Stalks and bunch

3. Lettuces and salad greens should be stored in protective containers at what temperature?
   a. 30–32 ° F.
   b. 32–34 ° F.
   c. 34–38 ° F.
   d. 40–50 ° F.

4. What type of an emulsion is a basic vinaigrette?
   a. Permanent
   b. Semi-permanent
   c. Temporary
   d. Semi-temporary

5. Approximately how much oil can one egg yolk emulsify?
   a. 2 ounces
   b. 4 ounces
   c. 1 cup
   d. 7 ounces

6. In a composed salad, the green would serve as the:
   a. base
   b. body
   c. garnish
   d. dressing

7. "Tomato and Asparagus Salad with Fresh Mozzarella" would be considered a:
   a. fruit salad
   b. composed salad
   c. vegetable salad
   d. bound salad

8. Traditional potato salad is considered a:
   a. green salad
   b. composed salad
   c. vegetable salad
   d. bound salad

9. Due to the flavor characteristics of mache, what *would not* be an appropriate green to toss with this in a salad?
   a. Boston lettuce
   b. Radiccchio
   c. Bibb lettuce
   d. Iceberg lettuce

24C. Short Answer

Provide a short response that correctly answers each of the questions below.

1. What are three (3) things that should be avoided when making a nutritionally balanced salad? The overuse of:

   a. _____

   b. _____

   c. _____

2. Give two (2) reasons why greens should be stored seperately from tomatoes and apples.

   a. _____

   b. _____

3. List five (5) of the ingredients that may be included in mayonnaise-based dressing.

   a. _____   d. _____

   b. _____   e. _____

   c. _____

4. Briefly describe the eight (8) basic steps to be followed when making mayonnaise.

   a. _____

   b. _____

   c. _____

   d. _____

   e. _____

f. _____

g. _____

h. _____

5. List four (4) possible ingredients for a fruit salad dressing:

a. _____   c. _____

b. _____   d. _____

24D. Chapter Review

For each question below, circle either True or False to indicate the correct answer.

1. The balance of vinegar, oil, lecithin and whipping is crucial to achieve a proper emulsion.
   True   False

2. Chicory, Belgian endive, sorrel, and spinach are all examples of salad greens that can be eaten raw or cooked.
   True   False

3. Romaine or cos lettuce benefits from hand-tearing to break it into smaller pieces, while butterhead and baby lettuces can be cut with a knife.
   True   False

4. Tossed salads should be dressed at the last possible moment before service to prevent over-marination from the dressing.
   True   False

5. Generally softer-leaved varieties of lettuces like Iceberg and red-leaf tend to perish more quickly in storage than crisper-leaved varieties.
   True   False

6. The best rule of thumb to follow when matching dressings to salad greens is, "the milder the flavor of the salad green, the milder the flavor of the dressing."
   True   False

7. All greens should be washed *after* they've been torn or cut.
   True   False

8. The standard ratio of oil to vinegar in a temporary emulsion is 2 parts to 1; however this ratio may vary when using strongly flavored oils, thus decreasing the proportion of oil to vinegar to 1 part oil to 1 part vinegar.
   True   False

9. Once washed, salad greens should be dried well to maintain a crisp texture and to ensure that oil-based dressings will adhere to the leaves.
   True   False

10. An advantage of using an emulsified vinaigrette dressing instead of a mayon-naise-based dressing is that it has the basic flavor of a vinaigrette without being as heavy as mayonnaise.
    True   False

TEST YOUR KNOWLEDGE

The practice sets provided below have been designed to test your comprehension of the information found in this chapter. It is recommended that you read the chapter completely before attempting these questions.

25A. Terminology

Fill in the blank spaces with the correct definition.

1. Ripened

   _____

2. Acidulation

   _____

3. Preserve

   _____

4. Pectin

   _____

5. Marmalade

   _____

6. Papain

   _____

7. Gel

   _____

8. Jam

   _____

9. Jelly

   _____

25B. Fill in the Blank

Fill in the blanks provided with the response that correctly answers the statement.

1. List the four (4) fruits that emit ethylene gas.

    a. _____   c. _____

    b. _____   d. _____

2. What is an indicator of cold damage to bananas?

    _____

3. Fruits are varied in their content of vitamins and minerals. Identify the fruits that are plentiful in the listed elements.

    Vitamin C   *Vitamin A*   *Potassium*

    1._____   1._____   1. _____

    2._____   2._____   2. _____

    3._____   3._____   3. _____

4. List four (4) uses for lower grades of fruit.

    a. _____   c. _____

    b. _____   d. _____

5. List five (5) methods of fruit preservation.

    a. _____   d. _____

    b. _____   e. _____

    c. _____

6. Name four (4) fruits that benefit from acidulation.

    a. _____   c. _____

    b. _____   d. _____

7. _____ is the most common method of cooking pears.
8. In classical dishes, the term *à la Normande* refers to the use of _____.
9. Pumpkins, cucumbers, and melons are all members of the _____ family.
10. _____ are the single largest fruit crop in the world.
11. When deep frying fruits, the best results are achieved by first dipping the fruit slices in _____ before submerging in the fat.
12. Name five (5) fruits that maintain their texture when sautéed.

    a. _____   d. _____

    b. _____   e. _____

    c. _____

25C. Product Identification

Match each fruit in List A with the appropriate letter in List B. Each choice in List B can only be used once.

List A	**List B**
_____ 1. Tangerines	a. A vegetable that is prepared as a fruit, using lots of sugar to offset tart flavor
_____ 2. Grapes	b. Also known as mandarins
_____ 3. Quince	c. Member of the gourd family
_____ 4. Lemons	d. Too astringent to eat raw, but great when cooked with sugar
_____ 5. Sour cherries	e. The single largest fruit crop in the world
_____ 6. Dates	f. Deep golden-yellow color and a full floral aroma when ripe
_____ 7. Rhubarb	g. Appear to be dried, but are actually fresh fruits cultivated since ancient times
_____ 8. Plantains	h. Unpleasant to eat raw, but great for flavoring savory foods and sweets
_____ 9. Star Fruits	i. Light to dark red and so acidic they are rarely eaten uncooked
_____ 10. Pomegranates	j. Concentrated juice is made into grenadine syrup
	k. Larger but not as sweet as bananas, often cooked as a starchy vegetable

25D. Chapter Review

For each question below, circle either True or False to indicate the correct answer.

1. Carry-over cooking occurs with fruit.
   True   False

2. The two primary methods of juicing are pressure and blending.
   True   False

3. Sulfur dioxide is added to dried fruits to maintain their flavor during storage.
   True   False

4. Freezing is the best method for preserving the fresh appearance of fruit.
   True   False

5. The highest grade of fruit is U.S. No 1.
   True   False

6. Pineapples don't ripen after picking.
   True   False

7. Irradiation maintains fruit's flavor and texture while slowing the ripening process.
   True   False

8. Papayas are also known as carambola.
   True   False

9. Tropical fruit flavors complement rich or spicy meat, fish, and poultry dishes.
   True   False

10. Papayas are ripe when a greater proportion of the skin is yellow rather than green.
    True   False

11. Red Delicious apples are good for making pies.
    True   False

12. Stone fruits such as mangoes are commonly dried, or made into liqueurs and brandies.
    True   False

13. Nutritionally speaking, fruits are low in protein and fat, high in fiber, and a good source of energy.
    True   False

14. Meat tenderizers often contain enzymes similar to those found naturally in the seeds of kiwis, papayas and passion fruit.
    True   False

15. Fresh fruits are sold by weight or count.
    True   False

16. Although canning makes fruit's texture soft, it has little or no effect on vitamins A, B, C and D.
    True   False

17. Fruits layed in a pan, sprinkled with a strudel topping, and then baked are called cobblers.
    True   False

CHAPTER 26

SANDWICHES

TEST YOUR KNOWLEDGE

The practice sets provided below have been designed to test your comprehension of the information found in this chapter. It is recommended that you read the chapter completely before attempting these questions.

26A. Terminology

Fill in the blank spaces with the correct definition.

1. Hot closed sandwiches _____

2. Hot open-faced sandwich _____

3. Cold closed sandwiches _____

4. Cold open-faced sandwiches _____

26B. Short Answer

Provide a short response that correctly answers each of the questions below.

1. The cardinal rule of food handling is; keep hot foods _____ and keep cold foods _____.
2. Sandwiches are especially prone to food-borne illness because of the use of high _____ foods.
3. The deadliest source of cross-contamination is _____ _____.
4. The three principal spreads are _____, _____, and _____.
5. Tuna salad is an example of a _____ salad.

6. Pizza is an example of a _____, _____ sandwich.
7. Name and describe the three (3) steps for sandwich preparation:

a. _____

_____

b. _____

_____

c. _____

_____

26C. Multiple Choice

For each question below, choose one response that correctly answers the question.

1. The purpose of a sandwich spread is to add
   a. flavor
   b. color
   c. texture
   d. none of the above
2. Which of the following is not a sandwich filling?
   a. Cheese
   b. Shellfish
   c. Vegetable puree
   d. Eggs
3. Monte Cristo sandwich is an example of which of the following sandwiches?
   a. Wrap
   b. Hot open-faced
   c. Multidecker
   d. Deep-fried
4. Which of the following is an example of a hot open-faced sandwich?
   a. Pizza
   b. Quesadillas
   c. Tacos
   d. Tea sandwiches

26D. Chapter Review

For each question below circle either True or False to indicate the correct answer.

1. Vegetable purees provide a barrier to prevent the bread from getting soggy.
   True   False

2. Ingredients for sandwiches should always be stored at room temperature.
   True   False

3. Chicken salad is an example of a spread.
   True   False

4. Tea sandwiches are a small version of a cold closed sandwich.
   True   False

5. Sandwich ingredients should be covered to prevent dehydration.
   True   False

6. Hamburgers are usually served closed so that the burger stays warm.
   True   False

CHAPTER 27

CHARCUTERIE

TEST YOUR KNOWLEDGE

The practice sets provided below have been designed to test your comprehension of the information found in this chapter. It is recommended that you read this chapter completely before attempting these questions.

27A. Terminology

Fill in the blank spaces with the correct definition.

1. Forcemeat   _____

2. Dominant meat   _____

3. Canadian bacon   _____

4. Collagen casings   _____

5. Pâté spice   _____

6. Liver terrines   _____

7. Smoker   _____

8. Country-style forcemeats   _____

9. Prosciutto   _____

10. Cold smoking   _____

11. Fat   _____

12. Vegetable terrines   _____

13. Panada _____

14. Mousse _____

15. Common bacon _____

16. Foie gras terrines _____

17. Hot smoking _____

18. Chopped chicken liver _____

19. Mousseline forcemeats _____

20. Curing salt _____

21. Dried or hard sausages _____

22. Boneless or formed hams _____

23. Westphalien ham _____

24. Fresh sausages _____

25. Basic forcemeats _____

26. Smoked and cooked
    sausages _____

27. Pâté _____

28. Country ham _____

29. Natural casings _____

30. Terrine _____

31. Pâtés en croûte _____

32. Fresh ham _____

33. Pancetta _____

34. Galantine _____

35. Brawns or aspic terrines _____

36. Rillette _____

37. Confit _____

38. Ballottine _____

27B. Short Answer

Provide a short response that correctly answers each of the questions below.

1. Name three (3) kinds of forcemeat that can be used to make a pâté en croûte.

   a. _____

   b. _____

   c. _____

2. If a forcemeat won't emulsify in a warm kitchen, what can be done?

   _____

3. Compare and contrast a galantine and a ballottine.

   galantine   **ballottine**

   a. _____   _____

   b. _____   _____

   c. _____   _____

   d. _____   _____

   e. _____   _____

   f. _____   _____

4. What are three (3) steps one can take to ensure proper emulsification of a forcemeat?

   a. _____

   b. _____

   c. _____

5. List five (5) reasons to use an aspic jelly.

   a. _____

   b. _____

   c. _____

   d. _____

   e. _____

27C. Multiple Choice

For each question below, choose the one response that correctly answers the question.

1. When making a forcemeat, ingredient as well as equipment temperatures should be kept at what temperature throughout preparation?
   a. below 40° F.
   b. as cold as possible
   c. room temperature, but not to exceed 60° F.
   d. 42°–45° F.

2. Which of the following is *false* about salt curing? It:
   a. inhibits bacterial growth
   b. dehydrates the food
   c. is quick and easy
   d. can take the place of cooking

3. Meat-based galantines, terrines, and pâtés en croûte should be cooked to an internal temperature of:
   a. 140° F.
   b. 125° F.
   c. 150° F.
   d. 160° F.

4. When meats are cold smoked, what process is usually performed prior to the smoking?
   a. salt curing and brining
   b. trimming
   c. barding
   d. marinating

5. What gives ham, bacon, and other smoked meats their pink color?
   a. red dye #7 is added to the curing process
   b. the meat is cooked to a medium rare state of doneness
   c. smoking, when done slowly, maintains the natural color of meats
   d. nitrites are added to the cure

6. Which of the statements is *false* about a panada?
   a. aids in emulsification
   b. adds significant flavor
   c. should not make up more than 20% of the forcemeat
   d. is a binder

27D. Matching

Match each of the terms in List A with the appropriate letter definition in List B. Each choice in List B can only be used once.

List A	List B
_____ 1. Mousse	a. Pâté cooked in pastry dough
_____ 2. Country-style forcemeat	b. A cooked, light, airy, delicately flavored forcemeat
_____ 3. Brawn	c. A poached dumpling of mousseline forcemeat

_____ 4. Forcemeat

d. Meat, fish, or poultry, bound, seasoned, with or without garnishes

_____ 5. Mousseline forcemeat

e. A terrine made from highly simmered gelatinous cuts of meat, wine, and flavoring

_____ 6. Pâté en croûte

f. A puree of fully cooked meats, poultry, game, fish, shellfish, or vegetables, lightened with cream and bound with aspic

_____ 7. Galantine

g. A whole poultry item boned, stuffed, and reshaped, poached and served cold

_____ 8. Quenelle

h. A deboned, stuffed poultry leg, poached or braised and usually served hot

_____ 9. Terrine

i. A hearty, highly seasoned, coarse textured forcemeat

j. A coarse forcemeat cooked in an earthenware mold

27E. Chapter Review

For each question below, circle either True or False to indicate the correct answer.

1. It is possible to make a vegetable mousseline forcemeat.
   True   False

2. The best type of mold to use to make a pâté en croûte is a metal loaf pan.
   True   False

3. Sausages are forcemeats stuffed into casings.
   True   False

4. Bechamel sauces are used as a primary binding agent in most styles of forcemeats.
   True   False

5. Pork bellies are usually made into bacon.
   True   False

6. When marinating forcemeat ingredients before grinding, the trend today is to marinate them for longer periods to kill bacteria.
   True   False

7. Galantines are always served cold.
   True   False

8. Any type of forcemeat can be used to make a terrine.
   True   False

9. A fresh ham is made from the hog's shoulder.
   True   False

10. After testing a forcemeat's texture and finding it too firm, a little egg white should be added to fix the problem.
    True   False

11. A mousseline forcemeat can be served hot or cold.
    True   False

12. Only hams made in rural areas can be called country hams; all others must be called country-style hams.
    True   False

13. Chopped chicken liver has a longer shelf life than a rillette.
    True   False

14. Brining and pickling are the same procedure.
    True   False

15. The stock used to make chaud-froid sauce often determines the color and flavor of the sauce.
    True   False

CHAPTER 28

HORS d'OEUVRES AND CANAPES

TEST YOUR KNOWLEDGE

The practice sets provided below have been designed to test your comprehension of the information found in this chapter. It is recommended that you read the chapter completely before attempting these questions.

28A. Terminology

Fill in the blank spaces with the correct definition.

For each of the Caviars listed below, describe the following:
  a. Price
  b. Source
  c. Consistency

1. Beluga caviar   _____

    a. _____

    b. _____

    c. _____

2. Osetra caviar   _____

    a. _____

    b. _____

    c. _____

3. Sevruga caviar _____

    a. _____

    b. _____

    c. _____

4. Pressed caviar _____

    a. _____

    b. _____

    c. _____

5. American Sturgeon caviar _____

    a. _____

    b. _____

    c. _____

6. Golden whitefish caviar _____

    a. _____

    b. _____

    c. _____

7. Lumpfish caviar _____

    a. _____

    b. _____

    c. _____

8. Salmon caviar _____

    a. _____

    b. _____

    c. _____

9. Malassol _____

10. Canape base _____

11. Canape spread _____

12. Canape garnishes _____

13. Barquette _____

14. Tartlet _____

15. Profiterole _____

16. Crudite _____

17. Sushi _____

18. Sashimi _____

19. Rumaki _____

20. Wonton skins _____

28B. Multiple Choice

For each question below, choose the one response that correctly answers the question.

1. Caviar is best stored at:
   a. 34° F
   b. 30° F
   c. 35° F
   d. 32° F

2. Connoisseurs prefer to serve caviar in which of the following utensils?
   a. glass
   b. china
   c. metal
   d. plastic

3. Which of the following fish is *not* used for sushi?
   a. ahi
   b. flounder
   c. sea bass
   d. salmon

4. Rice wine is also known as:
   a. Wasabi
   b. Mirin
   c. Shoyu
   d. Nori

28C. Fill in the Blank

Fill in the blank provided with the response that correctly completes the statement.

1. The three (3) main ingredients found in sushi are:

    a. _____

    b. _____

    c. _____

2. Small skewers holding a combination of meat, poultry, game, fish or vegetables are called _____.

3. Wontons can be steamed, but are more often _____ or _____.

4. If hors d'oeuvres are being served before a meal _____ portions per person per hour should be prepared, but if they are being served alone, _____ portions per person per hour will probably be needed.

5. The key to good sushi is the freshness of the fish, which should be no more than _____ day(s) out of the water.

28D. Short Answer

Provide a short response that correctly answers each of the questions below.

1. List the four (4) guidelines for preparing hors d'oeuvres.

    a. _____

    b. _____

    c. _____

    d. _____

2. List six (6) canapé spreads and an appropriate garnish for each.

    a. _____

    b. _____

    c. _____

    d. _____

    e. _____

    f. _____

3. Name and describe four (4) seasonings used in sushi.

    a. _____

    b. _____

    c. _____

    d. _____

4. Briefly describe the six (6) guidelines for preparing appetizers.

a. _____

b. _____

c. _____

d. _____

e. _____

f. _____

5. List the three (3) guidelines for preparing canape spreads.

a. _____

b. _____

c. _____

6. Describe the three (3) factors that indicate the freshness of caviar.

a. _____

b. _____

c. _____

28E. Matching

Match each of the ingredients in List A with the appropriate description in List B. Each item in List A can only be used once.

List A	List B
_____ 1. Nori	a. Japanese soy sauce, which is lighter and more delicate than the Chinese variety
_____ 2. Wasabi	b. Fresh ginger pickled in vinegar
_____ 3. Shoyu	c. A strong aromatic root, purchased as a green powder—sometimes called horseradish
	d. A dried seaweed, used to add flavor and to contain the rolled rice and other ingredients

28F. Chapter Review

For each question below, circle either True or False to indicate the correct answer.

1. An appetizer is usually served before lunch.
   True   False

2. Frozen caviar should only be used as a garnish.
   True   False

3. Most refrigerators are warmer than 32° F, therefore caviar should be stored on ice.
   True   False

4. Caviar should be served in a stainless steel bowl because it keeps it cooler than glass or plastic.
   True   False

5. The primary purpose of spreading the canape base with a little butter is to add flavor.
   True   False

6. Canapes are best stored over night in the refrigerator before service.
   True   False

7. The best quality caviar is always the most expensive.
   True   False

8. If properly handled, caviar will last up to two weeks before opening.
   True   False

9. Sushi is prepared by adding rice wine and other seasonings to long-grain rice.
   True   False

CHAPTER 29

PRINCIPLES OF THE BAKESHOP

TEST YOUR KNOWLEDGE

The practice sets provided below have been designed to test your comprehension of the information found in this chapter. It is recommended that you read the chapter completely before attempting these questions.

29A. Terminology

Fill in the blank spaces with the correct definition.

1. Conching   _____

2. Tapioca   _____

3. All-purpose flour   _____

4. Dough   _____

5. Gluten   _____

6. Hygroscopic   _____

7. Cooked syrups   _____

8. Chocolate liquor or mass   _____

9. Brandy   _____

10. Granulated sugar   _____

11. Nib   _____

12. Molasses   _____

13. Sugar syrup   _____

14. Emulsions   _____

15. Liqueur   _____

16. Cocoa powder   _____

17. Fermentation   _____

18. Extracts   _____

19. Turbinado sugar   _____

20. Gelatinization   _____

21. Wines   _____

22. Sucrose   _____

23. Refined/table sugar   _____

24. Raw sugar   _____

25. Bloom   _____

26. Simple syrup   _____

27. Interferents   _____

28. Mixing methods   _____

29. Liquor   _____

30. Gelatin   _____

31. Starch retrogradation   _____

32. Batter   _____

29B. Matching

Match each of the terms in List A with the appropriate letter in List B. Each choice in List B can only be used once.

List A	List B
_____ 1. Blending	a. Use a spoon or electric mixer with paddle attachment
_____ 2. Cutting	b. Use a whisk or electric mixer with whip attachment
_____ 3. Sifting	c. Use a rubber spatula

_____ 4. Whipping

_____ 5. Folding

_____ 6. Creaming
_____ 7. Beating
_____ 8. Kneading
_____ 9. Stirring

d. Use a spoon, rubber spatula, whisk, or electric mixer with paddle attachment

e. Use an electric mixer with paddle attachment on medium speed

f. Use a rotary or drum sifter or mesh strainer

g. Use a whisk, spoon, or rubber spatula

h. Use a flat cake spatula or metal spatula

i. Use pastry cutters, fingers, or an electric mixer with paddle attachment

j. Use hands or an electric mixer with dough hook attachment

29C. Multiple Choice

For each question below, choose the one response that correctly answers the question.

1. All fats are considered to be shortenings in baking because they tenderize the product and:
   a. leaven
   b. strengthen the gluten strands
   c. give good color
   d. shorten the gluten strands

2. Composite flours are:
   a. made from corn, soybeans, and rice
   b. categorized as non-wheat flours
   c. naturally high in protein
   d. made with the bran intact

3. Sanding sugar is primarily used for:
   a. a granulated sugar substitute
   b. making light, tender cakes
   c. decorating cookies and pastries
   d. making icings and glazes for decorating

4. The most frequently used and therefore the most important ingredient in the bakeshop is:
   a. granulated sugar
   b. wheat flour
   c. shortening
   d. yeast

5. Whole wheat flour, which includes the bran and germ, is also called:
   a. wheat germ
   b. composite flour
   c. whole flour
   d. graham flour

6. Which of the following is _false_ about the role of sugar and sweeteners in the bakeshop? They:
   a. act as a crisping agent
   b. serve as a preservative
   c. tenderize products
   d. act as a creaming agent

7. A baked good's final texture is determined by the rise, which is caused by the
_____, _____, and _____ in the
dough or batter.
   a. temperature, sugar, yeast
   b. protein, gluten, strands
   c. glutenin, gliadin, water
   d. carbon dioxide, air, steam

8. 160° F. is the temperature at which gluten, dairy, and egg proteins
   a. brown
   b. soften
   c. crystallize
   d. solidify

9. Which statement is *false* about cooked sugars?
   a. As sugar caramelizes, its sweetening power decreases.
   b. As water evaporates, the temperature of the sugar rises.
   c. As sugar caramelizes, its sweetening power increases.
   d. The sugar's temperature indicates its concentration.

10. A change in a baked good's texture and starch granule structure results in:
   a. staling
   b. browning
   c. leavening
   d. gluten development

11. _____is the brown powder left after the_____is removed.
   a. Unsweetened chocolate, sugar
   b. Cocoa powder, sugar
   c. Milk chocolate, dairy solids
   d. Cocoa powder, cocoa butter

12. Sugar is graded in the following manner:
   a. U.S. Grade No.1, No.2, No. 3, No.4
   b. There are no government standards regulating grade labels
   c. U.S. Grade Extra Fancy, Fancy, Good, Standard
   d. U.S. Superior Grade, Standard Grade, Good Grade

13. The purpose of a hydrometer is to:
   a. measure specific gravity and degrees of concentration
   b. show the temperature of sugar syrups
   c. determine doneness
   d. measure the amounts of sugar needed in sugar syrups

29D. Chapter Review

For each question below, circle either True or False to indicate the correct answer.

1. Self rising flour is bread flour with salt and baking powder added to it.
   True   False

2. Glutenin and gliadin contain the gluten necessary to create a quality dough or
batter.
   True   False

3. Chocolate did not exist in Europe as we know it today until Columbus brought the first cocoa beans back to Spain from the New World.
   True   False

4. Unsweetened chocolate is pure hardened cocoa butter.
   True   False

5. Most white chocolate products are not made from cocoa beans since they substitute vegetable oils for cocoa butter.
   True   False

6. Chocolate will melt just below body temperature.
   True   False

7. Gluten provides structure in dough by enabling the gases from fermentation to be retained.
   True   False

8. Flour derived from the portion of the endosperm closest to the germ is coarser.
   True   False

9. Whole wheat flour has a shorter shelf life due to its fat content.
   True   False

10. Unopened bags of flour can be stored anywhere as long as the location is relatively cool and free of moisture.
    True   False

11. Beets and sugar cane are the two main sources for sugar.
    True   False

12. Unsalted butter is usually preferred to salted butter in baking because the salt may interfere with the product formula.
    True   False

13. "Carryover" cooking is a phenomenon that occurs in the bakeshop as well as the kitchen.
    True   False

14. A batter generally contains more fat, sugar, and liquid than a dough.
    True   False

15. Fats are like other bakeshop ingredients in that they will combine completely with liquids.
    True   False

16. Shortenings are versatile and therefore oils may be substituted for solid shortening, regardless of what the recipe suggests.
    True   False

17. Granulated and sheet gelatin may be used interchangeably in a formula, providing the same weight is used of both ingredients.
    True   False

18. If vanilla beans develop a white coating while in storage, they have become contaminated with mold and should not be used.
    True   False

19. The milk solids in milk chocolate decrease its shelf life in comparison to other types of chocolate.
    True   False

20. All countries use similar refining processes for chocolate and therefore there is little difference in the resulting texture.
    True   False

CHAPTER 30

QUICK BREADS

TEST YOUR KNOWLEDGE

The practice sets provided below have been designed to test your comprehension of the information found in this chapter. It is recommended that you read the chapter completely before attempting these questions.

30A. Terminology

Fill in the blank spaces with the correct definition.

1. Streusel

_____

2. Biscuit method

_____

3. Single-acting
   baking powder

_____

4. Creaming method

_____

5. Tunneling

_____

6. Muffin method

_____

7. Double-acting
   baking powder

_____

30B. Short Answer

Provide a short response that correctly answers each of the questions below.

1. Suggest a reason why muffins might have a soapy or bitter taste.

_____

2. Why might a recipe call for both baking soda and baking powder?

_____

_____

3. What situation might call for the use of double acting baking powder?

_____

_____

4. What does the higher fat content in the creaming method do to the gluten in the mixture and therefore for the final product?

_____

_____

5. Explain why the fat is softened in recipes using the creaming method.

_____

_____

6. Suggest a reason for elongated holes running through the center of baked muffins.

_____

7. What is the basic difference between a scone and a biscuit?

_____

_____

30C. Chapter Review

For each question below, circle either True or False to indicate the correct answer.

1. Bread flour is used to make biscuits.
   True   False

2. The creaming method is comparable to the mixing method used for many butter cakes.
   True   False

3. Honey, molasses, fresh fruit, and buttermilk are all examples of acids that may be used with baking soda.
   True   False

4. Baking powder requires an acid ingredient in the formula in order to create the chemical reaction.
   True   False

5. Some quick breads use yeast as the leavening agent.
   True   False

6. Too much kneading toughens biscuits.
   True   False

7. Fats used in the muffin method should be in a solid form.
   True   False

8. The reason for a flat top on a loaf of banana bread is probably that the leavening agent was not sufficiently strong.
   True   False

9. When carbon dioxide is trapped within a batter or dough it expands when heated, causing the product to rise.
   True   False

10. Batters and doughs made with single-acting baking powder do not need to be baked immediately, as long as the product is refrigerated immediately.
    True   False

11. In order for baking soda to leaven, a batter or dough must be baked.
    True   False

12. Shortcakes are made using the muffin method.
    True   False

13. Pancakes and waffles are a type of quickbread.
    True   False

14. Waffle irons should be washed after each to maintain a sanitary cooking surface.
    True   False

CHAPTER 31

YEAST BREADS

TEST YOUR KNOWLEDGE

The practice sets provided below have been designed to test your comprehension of the information found in this chapter. It is recommended that you read the chapter completely before attempting these questions.

31A. Terminology

Fill in the blank spaces with the correct definition.

1. Fermentation   _____

2. Punching down   _____

3. Straight dough method   _____

4. Oven spring   _____

5. Slashing or docking   _____

6. Fresh yeast   _____

7. Wash   _____

8. Sponge method   _____

9. Proof box   _____

10. Rolled-in doughs   _____

11. Rounding   _____

12. Proofing   _____

13. Quick-rise dry yeast   _____

31B. Multiple Choice

For each question below, choose the one response that correctly answers the question.

1. Which is an example of a rich dough?
   a. Biscuits
   b. Italian bread
   c. Challah bread
   d. Muffins

2. Quick-rise dry yeast uses _____ water in order to activate the fermentation process.
   a. 138° F.
   b. 95° F.
   c. 100-110° F.
   d. 125-130° F.

3. When yeast is combined with carbohydrates, the result is alcohol and:
   a. oxygen
   b. gas
   c. carbon dioxide
   d. water

4. The disadvantage of using butter in roll-in doughs is that it:
   a. has a high moisture content
   b. cracks and breaks
   c. adds too much salt to the dough
   d. needs to be clarified before using

5. Yeast products should be cooled to approximately what temperature?
   a. 32-34° F
   b. 60-70° F
   c. 45-50° F
   d. 80-90° F

6. Which of the following is *not* important when considering the amount of flour used in a yeast bread?
   a. percentage of salt in the formula
   b. flour storage conditions
   c. humidity level
   d. measuring accuracy of other ingredients

7. Commercial baking yeast was not made available in stores until:
   a. 1654
   b. 1857
   c. 1910
   d. 1868

8. There are primarily two market forms of bakers' yeast. They are:
   a. compressed and active dry
   b. brewers and compressed
   c. quick-rise dry and instant
   d. fresh and compressed

9. The primary chemical function of rounding is to:
   a. smooth the dough into round balls
   b. stretch the gluten into a smooth coating
   c. help retain the gases from fermentation
   d. proof the dough

10. When is "punching" performed?
    a. After initial fermentation
    b. After proofing
    c. During proofing
    d. After initial mixing of dough

31C. Short Answer

Provide a short response that correctly answers each of the questions below.

1. Explain the two (2) steps involved in the sponge method.

    a. _____

    b. _____

2. Why is the organism in active dry yeast considered dormant?

    _____

3. List four (4) factors for determining the doneness of a baked yeast-leavened product.

    a. _____

    b. _____

    c. _____

    d. _____

4. List three (3) examples of a rolled-in dough product.

    a. _____ b. _____ c. _____

5. How is the quantity of dry yeast determined when it is being substituted for compressed yeast?

    _____

6. Describe the method for producing a straight method dough.

    _____

7. Briefly list the ten sequential stages of yeast bread production.

    a. _____   f. _____

    b. _____   g. _____

    c. _____   h. _____

    d. _____   i. _____

    e. _____   j. _____

31D. Chapter Review

For each question below, circle either True or False to indicate the correct answer.

1. Punching down occurs before the proofing process.
   True   False

2. Salt's primary role in bread making is seasoning.
   True   False

3. Italian bread is an example of a product made using the straight dough method.
   True   False

4. Washes can be applied before or after proofing occurs.
   True   False

5. Underproofing may result in a sour taste, poor volume, and a paler color after baking.
   True   False

6. Rich or rolled-in doughs are baked without steam.
   True   False

7. When properly stored, compressed yeast has a shelf life of two to three weeks.
   True   False

8. Active dry yeast contains approximately 10% moisture content.
   True   False

9. Instant yeast can be substituted measure for measure for regular dry yeast.
   True   False

10. Starters are used primarily for flavor in bread making.
    True   False

11. There is very little difference between the flavors of dry and compressed yeasts.
    True   False

12. Overkneading is a common problem in bread making.
    True   False

PIES, PASTRIES AND COOKIES

TEST YOUR KNOWLEDGE

The practice sets below have been designed to test your comprehension of the information found in this chapter. It is recommended that you read the chapter completely before attempting these questions.

32A. Terminology

Fill in the blank spaces with the correct definition.

1. Flaky dough _____

2. Pâte Sucrée _____

3. Meringue _____

4. Pâte à choux _____

5. Soft meringue _____

6. Paris-Brest _____

7. Wafer cookies _____

8. Cream filling _____

9. Mealy dough _____

10. Éclair paste _____

11. Italian meringue _____

12. Cream puffs _____

13. Bouchées _____

14. Sweet dough _____

15. Pie _____

16. Churros _____

17. Bar cookies _____

18. Hard meringue _____

19. Custard filling _____

20. Chiffon _____

21. Tart _____

22. Rolled/cut out cookies _____

23. Vol-au-vents _____

24. Crumbs _____

25. Common meringue _____

26. Puff pastry _____

27. Icebox cookies _____

28. Fruit fillings: cooked,
    cooked juice, baked _____

29. Detrempe _____

30. Swiss meringue _____

31. Baked blind _____

32. Pâte feuilletée _____

33. Crullers _____

34. Drop cookies _____

35. Beignets _____

36. Pressed cookies _____

37. Éclairs _____

38. Feuilletées _____

32B. Short Answer

Provide a short response that correctly answers each of the questions below.

1. List three (3) types of fillings that are used to fill prebaked pie crusts?

   a._____   c. _____

   b. _____

2. List four (4) types of fillings that are appropriate for filling a crumb crust.

   a._____   c. _____

   b. _____   d._____

3. Name two (2) types of fillings that are cooked by baking them *in* a crust.

   a._____   b. _____

4. List three (3) reasons for using a flaky dough to prepare pies.

   a._____   c. _____

   b. _____

5. Why is a sweet dough, or pâte sucrée, better for making tarts?

   _____

6. When is it appropriate to use a mealy crust?

   _____

7. Why is hand mixing best when making small to moderate quantities of flaky dough?

   _____

   _____

8. What makes pâte à choux unique among doughs?

   _____

   _____

9. What determines whether a meringue is hard or soft?

   _____

10. List four uses for puff pastry.

    a._____   c. _____

    b. _____   d._____

32C. Multiple Choice

For each question below, choose the one response that correctly answers the question.

1. What is the most common method for preparing cookie doughs?
   a. Beating
   b. Whipping
   c. Blending
   d. Creaming

2. Which is *not* a use for pâte a choux?
   a. Profiteroles
   b. Palmiers
   c. Éclairs
   d. Paris-Brest

3. What do all meringues have in common?
   a. The ratio of egg whites to sugar
   b. Whipped egg whites and sugar
   c. The flavoring ingredient used
   d. The method of preparation

4. Lacy pecan cookies are a cookie variety classified as a(n):
   a. pressed cookie
   b. icebox cookie
   c. wafer cookie
   d. drop cookie

5. Egg whites will whip better if _____ before whipping:
   a. a small amount of salt is added
   b. they are well chilled
   c. a portion of the sugar is added
   d. they are brought to room temperature

32D. Chapter Review

For each question below, circle either True or False to indicate the correct answer.

1. A baked meringue containing ground nuts is a dacquoise.
   True   False

2. Cherries and apples are appropriate fruits to use for a cooked juice filling.
   True   False

3. A cream filling is basically a flavored pastry cream.
   True   False

4. Pumpkin pie is a good example of a custard filling.
   True   False

5. The ratio for making a crumb crust is one part sugar, to four parts crumbs, to two parts melted butter.
   True   False

6. Rice or beans can be used for blind baking.
   True   False

7. Any dough can be used to make a tart shell as long as it tastes good and has a good appearance.
   True   False

8. Italian and Swiss meringues work equally well in buttercreams.
   True   False

9. A cooked juice filling should be combined with a raw crust and then baked.
   True   False

10. Baked fruit pies must be refrigerated to retard bacterial growth.
    True   False

11. The type of fat used in a flaky or mealy dough affects both the flavor and flakiness.
    True   False

12. An American gâteau is a pastry item made with puff pastry, éclair paste, short dough or sweet dough.
    True   False

CHAPTER 33

CAKES AND FROSTINGS

TEST YOUR KNOWLEDGE

The practice sets provided below have been designed to test your comprehension of the information found in this chapter. It is recommended that you read the chapter completely before attempting these questions.

33A. Terminology

Fill in the blank spaces with the correct definition.

1. Creamed fat _____

2. Whipping eggs _____

3. Butter cakes _____

4. Creaming method cakes _____

5. High-ratio cakes _____

6. Genoise _____

7. Spongecakes _____

8. Angel food cakes _____

9. Chiffon cakes _____

10. Icing _____

11. Buttercream _____

12. Foam _____

13. Fondant _____

14. Glaze _____

15. Royal icing _____

16. Ganach _____

17. Simple buttercream _____

18. Italian buttercream _____

19. French buttercream _____

20. Merangue buttercream _____

21. Mousseline buttercream _____

22. Boiled icing _____

23. Glucose _____

24. Flat icing _____

25. Decorator's icing _____

26. Side masking _____

27. Stencils _____

28. Baker's comb _____

33B. Basic Cake Mixes Revised

Describe the **basic** steps for the preparation of the following cake mixes and give a menu example of each type of cake. Number each step in the process for revision purposes. Exact quantities are not important for this exercise.

Example: **Chiffon Cake**

1.   Whip egg whites with a little sugar until stiff.
2.   Add liquid ingredients, including oil, to sifted dry ingredients.
3.   Fold in egg whites.
4.   Bake in ungreased pan.

Menu example: Lemon chiffon cake

I. Butter cake:

_____

_____

_____

_____

_____

II. High-ratio cake:

_____

_____

_____

_____

_____

III. Genoise cake:

_____

_____

_____

_____

_____

IV. Spongecake:

_____

_____

_____

_____

_____

V. Angel food cake:

_____

_____

_____

_____

_____

33C. Matching I - Ingredient Functions

Match each of the classification headings in List A with the appropriate ingredients in List B. Each choice in List B can only be used once.

List A

_____ 1. Flavoring
_____ 2. Toughener
_____ 3. Leavener
_____ 4. Tenderizer
_____ 5. Drier
_____ 6. Moistener

List B

a. Flour, milk, eggs
b. Flour, butter, water
c. Sugar, fats, yolks
d. Flour, starches, milk solids
e. Baking powder, baking soda
f. Cocoa, chocolate, spices, sour cream
g. Water, milk, juice, eggs

33D. Matching II - Frostings

Match each of the frostings in List A with the appropriate ingredients in List B. Each choice in List B can only be used once.

List A

_____ 1. Ganach
_____ 2. Fudge

_____ 3. Royal icing
_____ 4. Glaze
_____ 5. Buttercream
_____ 6. Fondant

List B

a. Sugar, fat, egg yolks or whites
b. Uncooked confectioner's sugar and egg whites
c. Merangue made with hot sugar syrup
d. Blend of melted chocolate and cream
e. Confectioner's sugar with liquid
f. Cooked mixture of sugar, butter and water/milk; applied warm
g. Cooked mixture of sugar and water, applied warm

33E. Cake Mixing Categories

Cake mixes fall into one of two categories: creamed fat or whipped egg. From the list below identify the creamed fat mixes with the letter **A** and the whipped egg mixes with the letter **B**.

A = Creamed Fat
B = Whipped Egg

_____ 1. Chiffon cake
_____ 2. Continental brownies
_____ 3. Devil's food cake
_____ 4. Chocolate spongecake
_____ 5. Sacher torte

_____ 6. Yellow cake
_____ 7. Carrot cake
_____ 8. Gateau Benoit
_____ 9. Vanilla raspberry layer cake
_____ 10. Sour cream coffeecake

33F. Frostings Revised

Describe the **basic** steps for the preparation of the following frostings. Number each step in the process for revision purposes. Exact quantities are not important for this exercise.

I. Simple buttercream

_____

_____

_____

_____

_____

II. Italian buttercream

_____

_____

_____

_____

_____

III. French Buttercream

_____

_____

_____

_____

_____

33G. Fill in the Blank

Fill in the blank with the response that correctly completes the statement.

1. The amount of leavening should be _____ at higher altitudes and the eggs in the mixture should be _____. Temperatures should also be _____ by _____ F at altitudes over 3,500 feet.
2. The three tests for determining a cakes doneness are a. _____, b. _____, and c. _____.
3. Most cakes are baked at temperatures between _____ and _____.
4. Royal icing is also known as _____.
5. Pan coating consists of equal parts _____ , _____ , and _____.

33H. Chapter Review

For each question below, circle True or False to indicate the correct answer.

1. The best way to cool a cake is to leave it in an area where there is a cool breeze.
   True   False

2. Frostings are not usually frozen.
   True   False

3. As a general guide for setting oven temperatures for cakes, the greater the surface area, the higher the temperature.
   True   False

4. When baking cakes, pans should be filled 1/2 to 3/4 with cake mix for the best results.
   True   False

5. Angel food cake is ideal for frosting.
   True   False

6. Solid shortening is better than butter for coating pans, since it does not contain any water.
   True   False

7. Package mixes are inferior in quality to cakes that are made from scratch.
   True   False

8. The fat used in high-ratio cake mixes can be either butter or shortening.
   True   False

CHAPTER 34

CUSTARDS, CREAMS, FROZEN DESSERTS AND DESSERT SAUCES

TEST YOUR KNOWLEDGE

The practice sets provided below have been designed to test your comprehension of the information found in this chapter. It is recommended that you read the chapter completely before attempting these questions.

34A. Terminology

Fill in the blank spaces with the correct definitions.

1. Custard _____

2. Stirred custard _____

3. Baked custard _____

4. Vanilla custard sauce _____

5. Pastry cream _____

6. Sabayon _____

7. Creme brulee _____

8. Mousseline _____

9. Creme chibouts _____

10. Temper _____

11. Creme caramel _____

12. Cheesecake _____

13. Bread pudding _____

14. Steep _____

15. Bavarian creams _____

16. Chiffons _____

17. Mousses _____

18. Cremes _____

19. Chantilly _____

20. Charlotte _____

21. Ice cream _____

22. Gelato _____

23. Sorbets _____

24. Sherbets _____

25. Semifreddi _____

26. Overrun _____

27. Sundae _____

28. Baked Alaska _____

29. Bombes _____

30. Coupes _____

31. Parfaits _____

32. Marquis _____

33. Neapolitans _____

34. Coulis _____

35. Base _____

36. Filling _____

37. Garnish _____

34B. Short Answer

Provide a short response that correctly answers the questions below.

1. Eggs are a high protein food and can easily be contaminated. List and describe the six (6) sanitary guidelines for handling eggs.

   a. _____

   b. _____

   c. _____

   d. _____

   e. _____

   f. _____

2. Describe the basic steps and essential ingredients for the preparation of vanilla custard sauce. Number each step in the process for revision purposes.

   Ingredients_____

   _____

   _____

   _____

   _____

   _____

   _____

   _____

3. Briefly describe the eight (8) sequential steps in the procedure for making ice cream.

   a. _____

   b. _____

   c. _____

   d. _____

   e. _____

   f. _____

   g. _____

   h. _____

4. Describe the four (4) sequential steps in the procedure for making baked souffles.

   a. _____

   b. _____

   c. _____

   d. _____

5. Describe the four (4) sequential steps in the procedure for making a sabayon.

   a. _____

   b. _____

   c. _____

   d. _____

6. Describe the three (3) sequential steps in the procedure for making a Mousse.

   a. _____

   b. _____

   c. _____

7. Briefly describe the nine (9) guidelines for assembling desserts.

   a. _____

   b. _____

   c. _____

   d. _____

   e. _____

   f. _____

   g. _____

   h. _____

   i. _____

34C. Fill in the Blank

Fill in the blanks with the response that correctly completes the statement.

1. _____ is another name for a sabayon.

2. Pastry cream can be lightened by folding in whipped cream to produce a _____ or by adding _____ to produce a crème Chiboust.

3. Some creams such as _____ and _____ are thickened with gelatin, but others such as _____ and _____ are not, and are therefore softer and lighter.

4. When preparing a soufflé the custard base and egg whites should be at room temperature because _____ _____ and _____ _____.

34D. Chapter Review

For each question below, circle True or False to indicate the correct answer.

1. Once a vanilla custard is curdled it should be discarded.
   True   False

2. A frozen soufflé is not really a soufflé in the true sense.
   True   False

3. A sherbet differs from a sorbet in that a sorbet contains milk or egg yolk for added creaminess.
   True   False

4. Still-frozen desserts have a shorter shelf life than churned products.
   True   False

5. A coulis is a fruit puree made from either fresh or individually quick frozen (IQF) fruits.
   True   False

6. Quiche is an example of a baked custard.
   True   False

Test Your Knowledge

The practice sets provided below have been designed to test your comprehension of the information found in this chapter. It is recommended that you read the chapter completely before attempting these questions.

35A. Terminology

Fill in the blank spaces with the correct definition.

1. Service _____

2. Composition _____

3. Presentation _____

35B. Fill in the Blank

Fill in the blanks provided with the response that correctly answers each statement.

1. _____ is a cookielike dough piped very thin and baked for use in making decorations and garnishes.
2. Proper cooking procedures can enhance the _____, _____, and _____ of many cooked foods.
3. List two (2) ways of presenting Polenta.

   a. _____

   b. _____

4. Once the color or pattern is chosen for a plate, the next important element to consider is _____, keeping in mind the amount of food being presented.

5. The _____ is often the highest point on the plate.
6. List five (5) things that a sauce should add to a plate presentation.

    a. _____   d. _____

    b. _____   e. _____

    c. _____

7. Plate drawing is most typically done with _____ sauces.
8. List two (2) things that a hippen masse garnish might do for a presentation.

    a. _____

    b. _____

9. List three (3) reasons for carefully cutting foods.

    a. _____

    b. _____

    c. _____

35C. Chapter Review

For each question below, circle either True or False to indicate the correct answer.

1. A rice pilaf is a good example of a dish that would mold well for an attractive presentation.
   True   False

2. The garnish should always be the focal point of the plate.
   True   False

3. Generally speaking, foods with similar textures look boring together.
   True   False

4. Dusting a plate can be done after the plating of the food is complete.
   True   False

5. A piping bag would be a good choice of equipment for performing sauce drawings.
   True   False

6. The primary consideration with sauce drawing is that the colors of the sauces used contrast each other.
   True   False

7. Properly preparing the main food product on a plate is the most important way to make the presentation look attractive.
   True   False

8. Plate dusting is a garnishing technique most associated with culinary preparations.
   True   False

CHAPTER 36

BUFFET PRESENTATION

TEST YOUR KNOWLEDGE

The practice sets provided below have been designed to test your comprehension of the information found in this chapter. It is recommended that you read the chapter completely before attempting these questions.

36A. Terminology

Fill in the blank spaces with the correct definition.

1. Theme _____

2. Menu _____

3. Chafing dish _____

4. Grosse piece _____

5. Risers _____

6. Butler service _____

36B. Short Answer

Provide a short response that correctly answers each of the questions below.

1. Describe the four (4) guidelines for avoiding repetition on a buffet.

   a. _____
      _____

   b. _____
      _____

c. _____
_____

d. _____
_____

2. Explain why each of the following aspects of presentation are important when preparing a buffet.

a. Height: _____
_____

b. Pattern: _____
_____

c. Color: _____
_____

d. Texture: _____
_____

e. Negative Space: _____
_____

3. Describe three (3) styles of buffet set-up designed to promote efficient service of large groups.

a. _____
_____

b. _____
_____

c. _____
_____

4. Describe four (4) guidelines for presenting *hot* foods on a buffet

a. _____
_____

b. _____
_____

c. _____
_____

d. _____
_____

36C. Multiple Choice

For each question below, choose the one response that correctly answers the question.

1. On a buffet, *hot* foods are served in/on:
   a. Platters
   b. Bowls
   c. Chafing dishes
   d. Mirrors
2. Which of the following best describes the logical flow for a buffet table?
   a. Appetizers, entrees, plates, vegetable
   b. Plates, soups, entrees, desserts
   c. Plates, entrees, vegetable, appetizers
   d. Desserts, vegetable, entrees, appetizers
3. Which of the following items are appropriate to use as a centerpiece on a buffet table?
   a. Flowers
   b. Ice carvings
   c. Whole turkey
   d. All of the above
4. Having waiters stationed behind the buffet table is called:
   a. Waiter service
   b. Buffet service
   c. Butler service
   d. Restaurant service

36D. Chapter Review

For each question below, circle either True or False to indicate the correct answer.

1. The word buffet is used to describe the event as well as the table on which the food is served.
   True   False

2. Cost is *not* a factor when preparing buffet menus.
   True   False

3. When designing a buffet, the food tables should be located as far away from the kitchen as possible for ease of service.
   True   False

4. The start of the buffet should be located near the entrance to the room.
   True   False

5. A buffet table with 10 items should measure approximately 10 feet long.
   True   False

6. Dishes containing sauces should be positioned at the back of the table.
   True   False

7. Dead space on the buffet should never be filled in with decorations or props.
   True   False

8. Guests will generally eat more at the beginning of the buffet than at the end.
   True   False

9. Spaghetti is an appropriate food to serve on a hot buffet.
   True   False

10. Dishes of food on the buffet should be replenished when they are two-thirds empty.
    True   False

Answers

Chapter 1

1A. Terminology

Answers will not be provided in answer key. All answers can be found in text.

1B. Fill in the Blank

1. Back of the house
2. French
3. Front of the house
4. Russian
5. Front waiter
6. American
7. Backwaiter or busperson

1C. Short Answer

1. a. Simultaneous cooking of many items, especially those needing constant and delicate attention
   b. Cooks could more comfortably and safely approach the heat source and control its temperatures
   c. Cooks could efficiently prepare and hold a multitude of smaller amounts of items requiring different cooking methods or ingredients for later use or service.
2. a. Canned foods
   b. Refrigerators
   c. Freezers
   d. Freeze-drying
   e. Vacuum-packing
   f. Irradiation
3. a. Absorbs facial perspiration
   b. Disguise stains
   c. Double-breasted design can be used to hide dirt and protects from scalds and burns

4. a. Age
   b. Type of household
   c. Income
   d. Education
   e. Geography
5. a. Personal performance and behavior
   b. Good grooming practices
   c. Clean, pressed uniform

1D. Defining Professionalism

1. Judgment
2. Dedication
3. Taste
4. Pride
5. Skill
6. Knowledge

1E. Matching

1. a   6. d
2. j   7. b
3. e   8. f
4. c   9. h
5. g   10. l

1F. Chapter Review

1. True (p. 13)
2. False (p. 11). Today most foodservice operations utilize a simplified version of Escoffier's kitchen brigade.
3. False (p. 9). Most new concerns that affect the foodservice industry are brought on by the demands of the customer. Such concerns may eventually encourage government interaction to ensure public well-being.
4. False (p. 8). Advances in the transportation industry began to positively influence the foodservice industry during the early 1800's.
5. False (p. 10). A regional cuisine is a set of recipes based upon local ingredients, traditions and practices.
6. False (p. 12). Restaurants offering buffet service generally charge by the meal; if they charge by the dish they are known as cafeterias.
7. True (p. 4)
8. True (p. 10)
9. True (p. 10)
10. False (p. 9). Many of the preserving techniques used prior to the 19th century destroyed or distorted the appearance and flavor the foods. Therefore, when new preserving techniques were developed in the early 19th century, many of them were adopted due to their minimal effect on appearance and flavor.
11. True (p. 14)
12. False (p. 10). Dining in a linear fashion does not allow for a full, simultaneous satisfaction of the groups of taste which, from a Western perspective, generally do not include spicy.

CHAPTER 2

2A. Terminology

Answers will not be provided in answer key. All answers can be found in text.

2B. Multiple Choice

1. d
2. d
3. b
4. d
5. c
6. b

2C. Chapter Review

1. True (p. 23)
2. False (p. 32). A licensed pest control operator should be contacted immediately. Such professionals will go beyond simply locating the source of infestation, but will also prescribe a plan of action to prevent ongoing occurrences in the future.
3. False (p. 22). Toxins cannot be smelled, seen, or tasted.
4. False (p. 23). Semisolid foods should be placed in containers that are less than 2 inches deep since increasing the surface area decreases the cooling time.
5. True (p. 29)
6. True (p. 30)
7. True (p. 32)
8. False (p. 29). Just as hands should be washed regularly during food production to prevent cross contamination, so too should gloves be changed regularly. Wearing gloves does not eliminate the need to wash hands regularly.
9. False (p. 26). Hepatitis A is a virus.
10. True (p. 23)

2D. Food-Borne Diseases Review

1. **Botulism**
   O: Clostridium botulinum
   F: Toxin, cells, spores
   S: Cooked foods held for an extended time at warm temperature with limited oxygen, rice, potatoes, smoked fish, canned vegetables
   P: Keep internal temperature of cooked foods above 140° F. or below 40° F; reheat leftovers thoroughly; discard swollen cans
2. **Hepatitis A**
   O: Virus
   S: Enters food supply through shellfish harvested from polluted waters. It is also carried by humans, often without knowledge of infection.
   P: Confirm source of shellfish, good personal hygiene, avoid cross-contamination.
3. **Strep**
   O: Streptococcus
   F: Cells
   S: Infected food workers
   P: Do not allow employees to work if ill; protect foods from customers' coughs and sneezes.

4. ***Perfringens or CP***
   O: Clostridium Perfringens
   F: Cells and toxin
   S: Reheated meats, sauces, stews, casseroles
   P: Keep cooked foods at an internal temperature of 140° F. or higher; reheat leftovers to internal temperature of 165° F. or higher

5. ***Norwalk Virus***
   O: Virus
   S: Spread almost entirely by poor personal hygiene of foodservice employees. It is found in human feces, contaminated water or vegetables fertilized with manure.
   P: The virus can be destroyed by high cooking temperatures but not by sanitizing solutions or freezing.

6. ***Salmonella***
   O: Salmonella
   F: Cells
   S: Poultry, eggs, milk, meats, fecal contamination
   P: Thoroughly cook all meat, poultry, fish and eggs; avoid cross-contamination with raw foods, maintain good personal hygiene.

7. ***E. Coli or 0157***
   O: Escherichia coli 0157:7
   F: Cells and toxins
   S: Any food, especially raw milk, raw vegetables, raw or rare beef, humans.
   P: Thoroughly cook or reheat items

8. ***Trichinosis***
   O: Parasitic worms
   S: Eating undercooked game or pork infected with trichina larvae.
   P: Cook foods to a minimum internal temperature of 137° F. for 10 seconds.

9. ***Anisakiasis***
   O: Parasitic roundworms
   S: The organs of fish, especially bottom feeders or those taken from contaminated waters. Raw or undercooked fish are often implicated.
   P: Fish should be thoroughly cleaned immediately after being caught so that the parasites do not have the opportunity to spread. Thoroughly cook to a minimum internal temperature of 140° F.

10. ***Listeriosis***
    O: Listeria Monocytogenes
    F: Cells
    S: Milk products, humans
    P: Avoid raw milk and cheese made from unpasteurized milk.

11. ***Staphylococcus***
    O: Staphylococcus Aureus
    F: Toxin
    S: Starchy foods, cold meats, bakery items, custards, milk products, humans with infected wounds or sores.
    P: Wash hands and utensils before use; exclude unhealthy food handlers; avoid having foods at room temperature.

Chapter 3

3A. Terminology

Answers will not be provided in answer key. All answers can be found in text.

3B. The Chef's Role in Nutrition

1. a. Use proper purchasing and storage techniques in order to preserve nutrients
   b. Offer a variety of foods from each tier of the Food pyramid so that customers have a choice
   c. Offer entrees that emphasize plant instead of animal foods
   d. Offer dishes that are considerate of special dietary needs such as low fat or low salt
   e. Use cooking procedures that preserve rather than destroy nutrients (see p. 55 for more)
2. For a professional perspective, see page 55, "The Customers Who Count".
3. a. Reduce the amounts of the ingredient(s)
   b. Replace the ingredient(s) with a substitute that will do the least to change the flavor and appearance of the dish
   c. Eliminate the ingredient(s)

3C. Parts of a Food Label

   a. serving size
   b. percent daily value
   c. calories per gram
   d. calories from fat
   e. recommended daily intake (RDI)
   f. daily values

3D. The Food Guide Pyramid

1. f   6. b
2. e   7. g
3. j   8. d
4. i   9. a
5. c

3E. Essential Nutrients

1. d
2. b
3. a
4. c

3F. Chapter Review

1. True (p. 54)
2. False (p. 45). RDA stands for Recommended Dietary Allowances.
3. True (p. 50)
4. True (p. 43)
5. True (p. 38)
6. False (p. 54). A chef should be able to prepare and serve food that meets the high standards for health demanded by some patrons, while maintaining the flavor and appearance important to everyone.
7. False (p. 40). Dietary cholesterol is found only in foods of animal origin.
8. False (p. 40). The body has more difficulty breaking down saturated fats.
9. True (p. 41)
10. False (p 48). Any artificial sweetener cannot be substituted for sugar when preparing baked goods. For instance, Aspartame breaks down when heated and therefore cannot be used to sweeten foods that will be cooked.

CHAPTER 4

4A. Terminology

Answers will not be provided in answer key. All answers can be found in text.

4B. Units of Measure

1. 16 oz
2. 28.35 g
3. 453.6 g = .4536 k / .5 k
4. 1,000 g
5. .035 oz
6. 35 oz = 2.187 lb / 2 lb
7. 16 tbsp = 8 fl oz
8. 1 qt = 32 fl oz
9. 1/2 gal = 4 pt
10. 16 tbsp = 8 fl oz

4C. Recipe Conversion

	Conversion Factor I .875	Yield I 28 Portions 6 oz each 168 oz	Conversion Factor II 1.5	Yield II 84 Portions 3 oz each 252 oz
Butter		3 oz		4 1/2 oz
Onion		10 1/2 oz		15 3/4 oz = 1 lb 4 oz
Celery		2 oz		3 oz
Broccoli		42 oz = 2 lb 10 oz		63 oz = 3 lb 15 oz
Chicken veloute		112 fl. oz = 3 1/2 qts		168 fl. oz = 5 1/4 qts
Chicken stock		56 fl. oz = 1 3/4 qts		84 fl. oz = 2 qts 20 fl. oz
Cream		21 fl. oz = 2 cups 5 fl. oz		31 1/2 fl. oz = 3 cups 7 1/2 fl. oz
Broccoli florets		7 oz		10 1/2 oz

4D. Conversion Problems

1. Larger quantities may require the use of a mixer versus hand mixing. Also the mixing time may need to be modified accordingly.
2. The difference in surface area between using a saucepan versus a tilting skillet impacts evaporation. Thickness of the liquid should be modified accordingly.
3. Some recipes may have errors. Read recipes carefully and draw on professional knowledge to compensate for such errors.
4. Cooking time of individual items should not vary according to volume. Cooking time will be affected by the evaporation rate due to equipment changes. Rely on professional knowledge to compensate for such changes.

4E. Unit Costs

1. $43.75	5. .26 cents
2. 85 cents	6. .25 cents
3. .56c	7. $3.25
4. $637.50	8. .15c

4F. Cost Per Portion

1. $4.50
2. $4.13
3. .25c
4. .75c

4G. Controlling Food Costs

1. The menu should be designed based upon customer desires, space, equipment, ingredient availability, cost of goods sold, employee skills and competition. Include all personnel when planning the menu.
2. Correct purchasing techniques help to control cost. Purchase specifications and periodic quotes help to insure value for money.
3. The person signing for the goods should be the person who actually checked them. Freshness, quality and quantity should always be checked.
4. Proper storage is crucial to prevent spoilage, pilferage and waste. Use the FIFO method.
5. Maintaining an ongoing inventory records sheets helps the ordering process and proper stock rotation.
6. Standardized portions are a key factor in controlling food cost. Once an acceptable portion size has been decided, it must be adhered to.
7. An accurate sales history helps to prevent over production, but the chef must also be able to use leftovers to lower food cost.
8. Front of the house personnel must be trained to avoid loss of sales due to free meals or spilled foods.

Chapter 5

5A. Terminology

Answers will not be provided in answer key. All answers can be found in text.

5B. Equipment Identification

1. **Equipment Name:** Zester
   Major Uses: Removing zest from citrus fruits
2. **Equipment Name:** Straight spatula (cake spatula)
   Major Uses: Applying frosting to cakes
3. **Equipment Name:** Grill spatula
   Major Uses: Lifting hot food items from pan or grill
4. **Equipment Name:** Meat mallet
   Major Uses: Flattening or tenderizing meat
5. **Equipment Name:** Chef's fork
   Major Uses: Carving meats
6. **Equipment Name:** French knife
   Major Uses: All purpose chopping
7. **Equipment Name:** Rigid boning knife
   Major Uses: Separating meat from bone
8. **Equipment Name:** Paring knife
   Major Uses: Detailed cutting of curved surfaces, namely vegetables
9. **Equipment Name:** Flexible slicer
   Major Uses: Slicing meats and fish
10. **Equipment Name:** Butcher knife or scimitar
    Major Uses: Fabricating raw meat
11. **Equipment Name:** Steel
    Major Uses: Honing blade between sharpenings
12. **Equipment Name:** Stockpot with spigot
    Major Uses: Making large quantities of soup or stock
13. **Equipment Name:** Rondeau / Brazier
    Major Uses: Stove top cooking for large amounts of food
14. **Equipment Name:** Sautoir
    Major Uses: Stove top cooking for small amounts of food
15. **Equipment Name:** Sauteuse
    Major Uses: Stove top cooking for sauteing
16. **Equipment Name:** Wok
    Major Uses: Stir-frying and sauteing
17. **Equipment Name:** Hotel pan
    Major Uses: Holding food during service, baking, roasting, poaching
18. **Equipment Name:** Drum sieve
    Major Uses: Sifting
19. **Equipment Name:** China cap
    Major Uses: Straining liquids
20. **Equipment Name:** Skimmer
    Major Uses: Skimming stocks

21. **Equipment Name:**   Spider
    Major Uses: Removing particles from liquids
22. **Equipment Name:**   Food mill
    Major Uses: Pureeing and straining foods
23. **Equipment Name:**   Mandoline
    Major Uses: Slicing small quantities of vegetables
24. **Equipment Name:**   Heavy duty blender
    Major Uses: Preparing smooth drinks and purees, chopping ice
25. **Equipment Name:**   Stack oven
    Major Uses: Baking
26. **Equipment Name:**   Tilting skillet
    Major Uses: A large cooking utensil that can be used as a stock-pot, brazier, fry pan, griddle or steam table.
27. **Equipment Name:**   Steam kettle
    Major Uses: Making stocks, soups, custards, or stocks
28. **Equipment Name:**   Deep-fat fryer
    Major Uses: Deep frying foods
29. **Equipment Name:**   Insulated carrier
    Major Uses: Keeping food hot during transportation

5C. Matching

1. i   6. d
2. h   7. c
3. a   8. f
4. e   9. j
5. g   10. k

5D. Short Answer

1. a. Easily cleaned
   b. Nontoxic food surfaces
   c. Smooth surfaces
   d. Smooth and sealed internal surfaces
   e. Nontoxic coating surfaces
   f. Easily cleaned
2. a. Is it necessary for production?
   b. Will it do the job in the space available?
   c. Is it the most economical for the establishment?
   d. Is it easy to clean and repair?
3. a. Carbon steel
   b. Stainless steel
   c. High carbon stainless steel

5E. Fill in the Blank

1. Utility   4. Buffalo chopper
2. Tang   5. Wooden
3. Griddle   6. Scimitar

5F. Calibrating a stem-type thermometer:

1. Fill a glass with shaved ice, then add water.
2. Place thermometer in the slush and wait until the temperature reading stabilizes. Following manufacturer's directions, adjust the thermometer's calibration nut until the temperature reads 32° F.
3. Check the calibration by returning the thermometer to the slush.
4. Repeat the procedure by substituting boiling water for the slush and calibrate the thermometer at 212° F.

5G. Chapter Review

1. False (p. 83). Stem-type thermomoters should be calibrated when dropped.
2. False (p. 95). Ventilation heads should be cleaned by professionals.
3. True (p. 85)
4. True (p. 95)
5. True (p. 80)
6. False (p. 93). Because a steam kettle heats the kettle's sides, it heats food more quickly than a pot sitting on a stove.

CHAPTER 6

6A. Terminology

Answers will not be provided in answer key. All answers can be found in text.

6B. Knife Safety

1. Think about what you are doing.
2. Always use the correct knife for the job.
3. Always cut away from yourself.
4. Always use a cutting board — never glass, marble or metal.
5. Keep knives sharp — a dull knife is more dangerous than a sharp one.
6. When carrying a knife, hold it point down.
7. Do not attempt to catch a falling knife — step back and allow it to fall.
8. Never leave a knife in a sink of water — anyone reaching into the sink may get cut.

6C. Cuts of Vegetables

1. 1/8 inch × 1/8 inch × 1 to 2 inches
2. 1/4 inch × 1/4 inch × 2 inches
3. 3/8 inch × 1/2 inch × 1/2 inch
4. 1/8 inch × 1/8 inch × 1/8 inch dice
5. 1/4 inch × 1/4 inch dice
6. 3/8 inch × 3/8 inch dice

Similarities: 1. Brunoise comes from julienne. 2. Small dice comes from batonnet.

6D. Fill in the Blank

1. Two
   Knife tip
   Wrist

2. Tip
   Rocking
3. Away
   Steel
   Glass
   Marble
4. Heel
   Coarsest
   Finest
5. Root

6E. Dicing an Onion

1. Remove the stem end with a paring knife, keeping the root intact. Peel off the outer skin without wasting too much.
2. Cut the onion in half through the stem and root.
3. Cut thin lines from the root towards the stem end, without cutting through the root.
4. Make as many cuts as possible through the width of the onion without cutting through the root.
5. Cut slices perpendicular to the other slices, producing diced onion.

6F. Chapter Review

1. False (p. 106)
2. True (p. 116)
3. False (p. 107). A steel does not sharpen a knife. Instead, it is used to hone or straighten the blade immediately after and between sharpenings.
4. False (p. 112)
5. False (p. 107). A whetstone can be moistened with either water or mineral oil, but not both.
6. True (p. 113)
7. True (p. 106)
8. True (p. 107)

CHAPTER 7

7A. Terminology

Answers will not be provided in answer key. All answers can be found in text.

7B. Categorizing Flavorings

herb	**spice**
1. Cilantro	6. Paprika
2. Oregano	7. Coriander
3. Lavender	8. Ground mustard
4. Thyme	9. Capers
5. Lemon grass	10. Black pepper

7C. Herbs and Spices

1. a
2. c
3. b
4. d
5. d
6. a
7. c
8. b
9. d
10. b

7D. Coffees and Teas

1. a. Body
   b. Smell
   c. Acidity
   d. Flavor
2. Arabica
3. Robusta
4. 2 Tablespoons, 6 ounces
5. Coffee
6. Tea
7. Black, Green, Oolong

7E. Chapter Review

1. False (p. 143). Green tea is yellow-green in color with a bitter flavor, but is not fermented at all.
2. True (p. 138)
3. True (p. 141)
4. False (p. 130). Use less dried herbs than you would fresh herbs in a recipe. The loss of moisture in the dried herbs supposedly strengthens and concentrates the flavors.
5. True (p. 130)
6. True (p. 138)
7. True (p. 132)
8. False (p. 142). Cafe latte is made by mixing 1/3 espresso and 2/3 steamed milk without foam.
9. True (p. 140)
10. True (p. 135)
11. True (p. 136)
12. False (p. 137). Distilled vinegar is made from grain alcohol.
13. False (p. 131). The presence of salt can be tasted easily but not smelled.
14. True (p. 130)

Chapter 8

8A. Terminology

Answers will not be provided in answer key. All answers can be found in text.

8B. Comparing Creams

1. e
2. d
3. b
4. a

8C. Cheese Identification

1. e	6. a	11. d	16. j
2. g	7. s	12. c	17. i
3. b	8. l	13. p	
4. m	9. r	14. n	
5. f	10. q	15. h	

8D. Milk Products

1. c	5. d
2. a	6. b
3. a	7. b
4. c	8. c

8E. Chapter Review

1. True (p. 149)
2. False (p. 153). Margarine is not made from animal products and therefore does not contain cholesterol.
3. True (p. 150)
4. False (p. 148). By law, all Grade A milk must be pasteurized prior to retail sale.
5. True (p. 150)
6. True (p. 152)
7. True (p. 152)
8. False (p. 151). Yogurt is only as healthful, or low in fat, as the milk it is made from.
9. False (p. 153). Margarine is not a dairy product and is included in this chapter only because it is so commonly used as a substitute for butter. It is actually made from animal or vegetable fats or a combination thereof. Flavorings, colorings, emulsifiers, preservatives, and vitamins are added before it is hydrogenated.
10. False (p. 161). Processed cheese food contains less natural cheese and more moisture than regular processed cheese. Often vegetable oil and milk solids are added to make the cheese food soft and spreadable.

11. True (p. 152)
12. True (p. 154)

Chapter 9

9A. Terminology

Answers will not be provided in answer key. All answers can be found in text.

9B. Cooking Methods

Cooking medium	Medium	Equipment
ex: *Sautéing*	*fat*	*stove*
1. Stewing	fat then liquid	stove (and oven), tilt skillet
2. Deep-fat frying	fat	deep fryer
3. Broiling	air	broiler, salamander, rotisserie
4. Poaching	water or other liquid	stove, oven, steam-jacketed kettle, tilt skillet
5. Grilling	air	grill
6. Simmering	water or other liquid	stove, steam-jacketed kettle, tilt skillet
7. Baking	air	oven
8. Roasting	air	oven
9. Steaming	steam	stove, convection steamer
10. Braising	fat then liquid	stove (and oven), tilt skillet

9C. Multiple Choice

1. a
2. d
3. c
4. a
5. c
6. b
7. d
8. c

9D. Short Answer

1. Braising
   a. Large pieces of food
   b. Brown then simmer/steam
   c. Cooking liquid covers 1/3-1/2
   d. Cooking time is longer (large pieces)

   Stewing
   a. Smaller pieces of food
   b. Brown or blanch then simmer/steam
   c. Cooking liquid completely covers
   d. Cooking time is shorter (small pieces)

2. a. The food product must be placed in a basket or on a rack to allow for circulation of the steam.
   b. A lid should cover the steaming unit to trap steam and allow heat to build up.

3. a. Heat a sauté pan over high heat
   b. Add a small amount of fat and heat until just below smoking point
   c. Add dry, seasoned chicken breast (or dredge in seasoned flour), placing in a single layer and presentation side down first
   d. Adjust temperature as needed to control browning, flip when half cooked
   e. Test for proper doneness, remove from pan, and serve as requested
4. a. Bring liquid to a boil in an appropriate pan.
   b. Add food product to the cooking liquid.
   c. Adjust the temperature to a gentle simmer (160° F. to 180° F.).
   d. Test the product for desired doneness.
   e. If desired, use poaching liquid to make sauce that will be served with the final dish.
   f. Serve with appropriate sauce and accompaniments.

9E. Matching

1. e
2. c
3. b
4. a
5. d
6. g

9F. Chapter Review

1. True (p. 170)
2. False (p. 170). Heat is generated quickly and uniformly throughout the food. Microwave cooking does not brown foods, however, and often gives meats a dry, mushy texture, making microwave ovens an unacceptable replacement for traditional ovens.
3. True (p. 169)
4. False (p. 169). A wood fired grill is an example of the radiation heat transfer method.
5. True (p. 174)
6. False (p. 173). In broiling the heat source comes from above the cooking surface.
7. False (p. 172). Deep frying is an example of a dry heat cooking method.
8. True (p. 173)
9. False (p. 174). Stir-frying is a variation in technique to sauteing but it does not necessarily use any additional fat in the process.
10. False (p. 175). A court bouillon should be used when poaching or simmering foods.
11. True (p. 177)
12. True (p. 177)

CHAPTER 10

10A. Terminology

Answers will not be provided in answer key. All answers can be found in text.

10B. Stock Making Review

White stock; Reference: page 184
Brown stock; Reference: page 186
Fish stock; Reference: page 187

10C. Sauce Review—Mother Sauces

Mother Sauce	Thickener	Liquid
1. Béchamel	White roux	Milk
2. Velouté	Blond roux	White/chicken/veal/fish stock
3. Espagnole	Brown roux	Beef stock
4. Tomato	Tomato purée	White stock
5. Hollandaise	Eggs	Butter

10D. Small Sauces

Mother Sauce	Ingredients Added
1. Bechamel	Scalded cream, lemon juice
2. Bechamel	Cheddar, Worcestershire sauce, dry mustard
3. Bechamel	Gruyere, Parmesan, scalded cream, butter
4. Bechamel	Heavy cream, crayfish butter, paprika, crayfish meat
5. Bechamel	Onion, sweated, cook and strain sauce
6. Chicken/veal veloute	Lemon juice and a liaison
7. Chicken veloute	Cream
8. Fish veloute	Diced shallots, dry white wine, butter and parsley
9. Fish veloute	Heavy cream, cayenne pepper, lobster butter, lobster coral
10. Fish veloute	Mushroom, liaison, strained
11. Chicken/veal veloute	Sauce Allemande, tomato paste, butter
12. Chicken/veal veloute	Sauce Allemande, heavy cream, mustard, horseradish
13. Chicken/veal veloute	Sauce Allemande, mushroom, shallots, cream, lemon juice, parsley
14. Chicken veloute	Sauce Supreme, glace de volaille, red pepper butter
15. Chicken veloute	Sauce Supreme, onion, butter, paprika, strain
16. Chicken veloute	Sauce Supreme, glace de volaille
17. Espagnole	Demi-glace, red wine, shallots, bay leaf, thyme, black pepper, butter, sliced poached beef marrow
18. Espagnole	Demi-glace, mushrooms, shallots, white wine, diced tomatoes, parsley
19. Espagnole	Demi-glace, white wine, shallots, lemon juice, cayenne pepper, tarragon

20. Espagnole	Poivrade sauce, (with bacon trimmings added to mirepoix), red wine, dash of cayenne
21. Espagnole	Demi-glace, madeira wine or ruby port
22. Espagnole	Demi-glace, red wine, shallots, strain
23. Espagnole	Demi-glace, truffles
24. Espagnole	Demi-glace, shallots, white wine, white wine vinegar, cornichons, tarragon, parsley, chervil
25. Espagnole	Demi-glace, mirepoix, bouquet garni, vinegar, white wine, crushed peppercorns, butter, strain
26. Espagnole	Demi-glace, onion, white wine, Dijon mustard, sugar, sliced pickles
27. Tomato sauce	Onion, celery, garlic, bay leaf, thyme, green pepper, hot pepper sauce
28. Tomato sauce	Mushroom, cooked ham, cooked tongue
29. Tomato sauce	Mushroom, onion, sliced black or green olives
30. Hollandaise	Shallots, tarragon, chervil, crushed peppercorns, white wine vinegar, cayenne pepper. Garnish: tarragon
31. Hollandaise	Bearnaise sauce, tomato paste, heavy cream
32. Hollandaise	Bearnaise sauce, glace de viande
33. Hollandaise	Infuse with saffron
34. Hollandaise	Orange juice, orange zest - blood oranges are traditional
35. Hollandaise	Heavy cream

10E. Short Answer

1.   a. Start the stock in **cold** water.
   b. **Simmer** the stock gently.
   c. **Skim** the stock frequently.
   d. **Strain** the stock carefully.
   e. **Cool** the stock quickly.
   f. **Store** the stock properly.
   g. **Degrease** the stock.
2. Hollandaise preparation: Reference p. 206 & 207
3.   a. Incorrect temperature of eggs and/or butter.
   b. Butter added too quickly.
   c. Egg yolks overcooked.
   d. Too much butter added.
   e. Sauce not whipped enough.
4. Reference pp. 194 & 195

10F. Matching

1. D, K, N
2. B, I, L
3. A, F, J
4. C, G, M
5. E, H, O

10G. Chapter Review

1. True (p. 192)
2. False (p. 194). To prevent lumps when making sauces add 1. cold stock to hot roux or 2. room-temperature roux to hot stock.
3. False (p. 195). Temperatures over 185° F. will cause the yolks to curdle.
4. True (p. 192)
5. True (p. 195)
6. True (p. 198)
7. False (p. 195). Tempering gradually raises the temperature of a cold liquid such as a liaison, by adding hot liquid.
8. True (p. 196)
9. True (p. 196)
10. False (p. 188). Fish stock should only simmer for 30 minutes.

CHAPTER 11

11A. Terminology

Answers will not be provided in answer key. All answers can be found in text.

11B. Broth Preparation Review

Reference p. 233

11C. Consomme Preparation Review I

Reference p. 236

11D. Consommé Preparation Review II

1. If the consommé is allowed to boil, or if it is stirred after the raft has been formed.
2. Stock was not degreased.
3. Poor quality stock.
4. Onion brulée omitted.

11E. Consomme Preparation Review III

1. Thoroughly chill and degrease the consomme
2. Lightly beat four egg whites per gallon of consomme and conbine with the cold consomme.
3. Slowly bring the consomme to a simmer, stirring occasionally. Stop stirring when the egg whites begin to coagulate.
4. When the egg whites are completely coagulated, carefully strain the consomme.

11F. Cream Soup Preparation Review

Reference p. 238

11G. Short Answer

1. a. Never add cold milk or cream to hot soup.
    b. Add milk or cream just before service.
    c. Do not boil soup after cream has been added.
2. Seven common categories of soup: Reference p. 232
3. a. Beef broth and consommé both have the same base—beef stock; however, beef broth uses meat and vegetables to give it a fuller flavor and consommé uses a clarif.
    Beef broth is not served as a clear soup, but consommé must be served clear.
    b. A cream of mushroom soup uses a roux to thicken the soup, but lentil soup uses a puree of the vegetable to thicken the soup.
    They may both use stock to form the base for flavor and both may use cream to finish the soup.
    A cream of mushroom soup is usually strained before service, whereas the lentil soup is usually not.
    c. Both are cold soups, however gazpacho uses uncooked ingredients and the cold consommé uses cooked ingredients and then cools them for service.

11H. Chapter Review

1. True (p. 240)
2. True (p. 238)
3. True (p. 236)
4. False (p. 236). A consommé is a clarified broth.
5. False (p. 238). Cream soups are thickened with a roux or other starch.
6. False (p. 233). Additional items added to the soup are always referred to as garnishes, therefore the onion in french onion soup is also a garnish.
7. False (p. 244). Cold soups should be served as cold as possible.
8. False (p. 238). If the consommé is insufficiently clear, a clarification can be performed.
9. False (p. 245). Cold dulls the sense of taste, therefore more seasoning is required.
10. True (p. 248)

CHAPTER 12

12A. Terminology

Answers will not be provided in answer key. All answers can be found in text.

12B. Fill in the Blank

1. Good quality
2. Low   long
3. Soft   very red
    Firm   non-red
4. Dredged in flour
5. Carryover
    Retain more juices
6. barding, larding

7. flavor, connective tissue
8. insects, bacteria, parasites
9. tough
10. against

12C. Matching

1. d
2. e
3. f
4. b
5. c

12D. Short Answer

Reference pp. 271–290

12E. Chapter Review

1. False (p. 269). Fresh meats should be stored at 30–35 degrees F.
2. False (p. 268). Green meats are meats that are frozen before rigor mortis has had an opportunity to dissipate.
3. True (p. 284)
4. True (p. 266). The USDA stamp only insures that the meat is processed in a sanitary way.
5. False (p. 266). USDA *prime cuts* are used for the finest establishments.
6. False (p. 267). Yield grades apply only to lamb and beef.
7. True (p. 268)
8. True (p. 268)
9. False (p. 264). Meat will hold in a vacuum package for up to six weeks under refrigeration.
10. True (p. 270)

CHAPTER 13

13A. Terminology

Answers will not be provided in answer key. All answers can be found in text.

13B. Primal Cuts of Beef

1. Chuck
2. Rib
3. Short loin
4. Sirloin
5. Round
6. Flank
7. Short plate
8. Brisket and shank

13C. Cuts from the Round

Subprimal/Fabricated Cut	Cooking Process/Use
1. Inside (top) round	Roast
2. Eye round	Braise
3. Outside (bottom) round	Braise
4. Knuckle or tip	Roast
5. Leg or round bone	Simmering—stocks, soups, consommé

13D. Cuts of Beef and Applied Cooking Methods

Cooking Method	Subprimal/Fabricated Cut	Primal Cut
1. Combination (braise/stew)	Chuck	Chuck
2. Combination (braise)	Shank	Brisket & shank
3. Dry heat (broil/grill/roast/saute)	Strip loin	Short loin
4. Dry heat (broil/grill/roast)	Ground beef	Chuck
5. Combination (braise)	Flank steak	Flank
6. Moist heat (simmer)	Brisket	Brisket & shank
7. Dry heat (broil/grill/roast)	Tenderloin	Short loin
8. Dry heat (broil/grill)	Flank steak	Flank
9. Dry heat (broil/grill/roast)	Tenderloin	Short loin
10. Dry heat (roast)	Steamship/top round	Round
11. Combination (braise)	Top round	Round
12. Dry heat (broil/grill)	Skirt steak	Short plate
13. Combination (stew)	Stew meat	Chuck
14. Combination (braise/stew)	Ground beef	Chuck
15. Dry heat (broil/grill/roast/saute)	Strip loin	Short loin

13E. Multiple Choice

1. b
2. c
3. d
4. a

13F. Matching I

1. c
2. e
3. a
4. b

13G. Matching II

a. 3	d. 2
b. 1	e. 1
c. 2	f. 3

13H. Chapter Review

1. False (p. 297). The hanging tenderloin is part a part of the flank that is particularly tender.
2. False (p. 294). The chuck has a high proportion of connective tissue which makes it more flavorful than the tenderloin.
3. True (p. 297)
4. False (p. 296). Prime rib refers to the fact that the rib is made up of the majority of the primal cut from which it comes.
5. True (p. 297)
6. True (p. 297)
7. True
8. False (p. 296). Pastrami is made by curing and peppering the brisket.

CHAPTER 14

14A. Terminology

Answers will not be provided in answer key. All answers can be found in text.

14B. Primal Cuts of Veal

1. Shoulder
2. Rib
3. Loin
4. Leg
5. Foreshank and breast

14C. Cuts of Veal and Applied Cooking Methods

	Cooking Method	Subprimal/ Fabricated Cut	Primal Cut
1.	Combination (stew)	Cubed veal	Shoulder
2.	Dry heat (broil/grill/roast)	Rib eye	Rib
3.	Combination (braise)	Breast	Foreshank & breast
4.	Dry heat (broil/grill/saute)	Loin chops	Loin
5.	Combination (stew)	Cubed veal	Shoulder
6.	Combination (braise)	Sweetbreads	Offal
7.	Combination (braise)	Kidneys	Offal
8.	Dry heat (broil/grill)	Ground veal	Shoulder
9.	Combination (braise)	Ground veal	Shoulder
10.	Dry heat (broil/grill/roast/saute)	Veal tenderloin	Loin
11.	Dry heat (roast/saute)	Top round	Leg
12.	Dry heat (broil/grill/saute)	Calves liver	Offal
13.	Combination (braise)	Hind/Foreshank	Leg/Foreshank & breast
14.	Dry heat (roast/saute)	Leg	Leg
15.	Moist heat (simmer	Hindshank	Leg

14D. Short Answer

1. a. Remove the shank
   b. Remove the butt tenderloin
   c. Remove the pelvic bone
   d. Remove the top round
   e. Remove the shank meat
   f. Remove the round bone and knuckle
   g. Remove the sirloin
   h. Remove the eye round
2. a. Top round
   b. Eye round
   c. Knuckle
   d. Sirloin
   e. Bottom round
   f. Butt tenderloin

3. ***Primal   Subprimal/Fabricated Cut   Menu Example***
   Ribs:

a.	Hotel rack	Roast veal with porcini mushrooms
b.	Rib chops	Braised veal chop with risotto
c.	Rib eye	Broiled rib eye with chipolte sauce

   Any three of the following would be appropriate answers:
   Loin:

a.	Veal loin	Roasted veal loin with wild mushrooms
b.	Loin chops	Sautéd veal chops with mushroom sauce
c.	Boneless strip loin	Roasted veal loin sauce poulette
d.	Veal tenderloin	Sautéed tenderloin with garlic and herbs

4. Reference: page 314.

14E. Matching I

1. f
2. a
3. b *d is appropriate for the breast only
4. e
5. c

14F. Matching II

a.	2	d.	2
b.	1	e.	1
c.	3	f.	3

14G. Chapter Review

1. True (p. 320)
2. True (p. 314)
3. False (p. 322). Sweetbreads are pressed to improve their texture.
4. False (p. 320). Émincé should be cut across the grain.
5. True (p. 317)
6. False (p. 317). The thymus glands shrink in older animals.
7. True (p. 317)
8. True (p. 317)

CHAPTER 15

15A. Terminology

Answers will not be provided in answer key. All answers can be found in text.

15B. Primal Cuts of Lamb

1. Shoulder
2. Rack
3. Loin
4. Leg
5. Breast

15C. Subprimal or Fabricated Cuts

Primal Cut	Subprimal/Fabricated Cuts	Cooking Methods
1.	a. Chops	Broil/grill
	b. Diced/ground	Stew/grill
2.	a. Chops	Grill
	b. Lamb rack	Roasted
3.	a. Chops/boneless roast	Grill/roast
	b. Medallions/noisettes	Sauté
4.	a. Lamb leg (bone-in)	Braised
	b. Boned leg	Roast
5.	a. Breast	Braise
	b. Lamb shanks	Braise

15D. Cuts of Lamb and Applied Cooking Methods

Cooking Method	Subprimal/ Fabricated Cut	Primal Cut
1. Broil/grill/roast	Loin chops	Loin
2. Stew	Diced lamb	Shoulder
3. Broil/grill/roast/sauté	Lamb loin	Loin
4. Stew	Diced lamb	Shoulder
5. Broil/grill/roast/sauté	Frenched lamb rack	Hotel rack
6. Combination (Braise)	Breast	Breast

7.	Dry heat (broil/grill/ roast/saute)		Lamb rack	Hotel rack
8.	Dry heat (roast)		Lamb leg	Leg

15E. Short Answer

1. Reference: Page 339
2. Reference: Page 340
3. Reference: Page 340

15F. Chapter Review

1. False (p. 336). Lamb primals are not classified into a forequarter and hindquarter as with beef, or a foresaddle and hindsaddle as with veal.
2. False (p. 336). Spring lamb is the term used to describe young lamb that has not been fed on grass or grains.
3. True (p. 336)
4. True (p. 338)
5. True (p. 338)
6. False (p. 332). The chine bone runs through the primal lamb rack.
7. True (p. 340)
8. True (p. 336)

CHAPTER 16

16A. Terminology

Answers will not be provided in answer key. All answers can be found in text.

16B. Primal Cuts of Pork

1. Boston butt
2. Loin
3. Fresh ham
4. Belly
5. Shoulder

16C. Subprimal or Fabricated Cuts

Primal Cut	Subprimal/ Fabricated Cut	Cooking Methods	Cured & Smoked	Fresh
1.	Boston butt	Broil/grill/sauté	X	X
2.	Pork back ribs	Steam—grill		X
	Pork loin chops	Broil/grill		X
	Pork tenderloin	Sauté/roast/braise/broil/grill		X
	Pork loin	Roast/braise		X
3.	Fresh ham	Roast/boil	X	X
4.	Spare ribs	Simmer—grill	X	X
	Bacon	Sauté/grill	X	
5.	Picnic shoulder	Bake	X	X

16D. Cuts of Pork and Applied Cooking Methods

Cooking Method	Subprimal/ Fabricated Cut	Primal Cut
1. Dry heat (roast)	Fresh ham	Fresh ham
2. Moist heat (simmer)	Boston butt	Boston butt
3. Dry heat (broil/grill/saute/roast)	Pork tenderloin	Loin
4. Combination (braise)	Pork loin	Loin
5. Combination (steam - grill)	Spare ribs	Belly
6. Dry heat (roast/bake)	Picnic shoulder	Shoulder
7. Dry heat (saute)	Bacon	Belly

16E. Short Answer

1. Reference: Page 364
2. a. Shoulder
   b. Shoulder hock
   c. Boston butt—cottage ham
   d. Spare ribs—belly
   e. Pork belly—bacon
   f. Boneless pork loin—Canadian bacon
   g. Fresh ham

16F. Matching

1. d
2. f
3. a
4. b
5. c

16G. Chapter Review

1. False (p. 360). The Boston butt is located in the forequarter.
2. True (p. 360)
3. True (p. 363)
4. False (p. 360). The foreshank is called the shoulder hock.
5. False (p. 363). Center-cut pork chops are the choicest chops from the primal loin.
6. False (p. 363). Canadian is made from the boneless pork loin.
7. True (p. 363)
8. True (p. 362)
9. False (p. 360)
10. False (p. 360)

CHAPTER 17

17A. Terminology

Answers will not be provided in answer key. All answers can be found in text.

17B. Short Answer

1. Reference: Page 397
2. Similarity: Overused muscles are more tough than underused ones.
   Difference: Red meat has marbling—poultry does not.
3. Reference: Page 384
4. Reference: Page 378
5. Chicken, duck, goose, guinea, pigeon, and turkey.
7. a. Be sure all work surfaces and equipment are clean.
   b. Avoid getting poultry juices in contact with other food.
   c. Anything coming in contact with raw poultry should be sanitized before it comes in contact with any other food.
   d. Cooked foods should never be placed in containers that were used to hold the raw product.
   e. Kitchen towels used to handle poultry should be sanitized before being reused to prevent cross-contamination.
8. Reference: Page 386 & 387

17C. Matching

1. b
2. e
3. a
4. f
5. c

17D. Fill in the Blank

1. Protein
   Myoglobin
2. 165 and 170° F
3. Roaster duckling
   Dark
   Fat
4. White wine or lemon, oil, salt, pepper, herbs and spices.
   Barbecue sauce

17E. Multiple Choice

1. c
2. b
3. a

17F. Chapter Review

1. False (p. 378). Poultry fat has a lower melting point than other animal fats.
2. True (p. 395)
3. True (p. 379)
4. False (p. 391). Poultry that is left too long in an acidic marinade may take on undesirable flavors.
5. False (p. 379). The cooking time for dark meat is longer.

6. False (p. 384). Poultry should be frozen at –18° C/0° F or below.
7. False (p. 379). The skin color of poultry is related to what it is fed.
8. True (p. 384)
9. False (p. 379). Older male birds have less flavor than older female birds.
10. False (p. 383). Overcooking foie gras will cause it to melt away.
11. False (p. 381). A young pigeon is known as a squab.
12. False (p. 382). The gizzard is the bird's stomach.
13. False (p. 379)
14. False (p. 379)
15. True (p. 382)
16. False (p. 382)
17. True (p. 391)
18. False (p. 391)
19. False (p. 392)
20. True (p. 384)

CHAPTER 18

18A. Terminology

Answers will not be provided in answer key. All answers can be found in text.

18B. Short Answer

1. a. sausages
   b. forcemeats
   c. pâtés
2. Reference: Page 438
3. Reference: Page 433
4. Reference: Page 438

18C. Multiple Choice

1. b
2. c
3. b
4. a
5. d
6. c

18D. Chapter Review

1. True (p. 437)
2. True (p. 437)
3. False (p. 434). Mature boar is one or two years old.
4. False (p. 438). Wild game can only be served by those who hunt and share their kill.
5. True (p. 434)
6. False (p. 437). Game is lower in fat and higher in protein and minerals than other meats.

7. False (p. 433). There is no marbling in venison flesh.
8. False (p. 432). Large game animals are available only precut into subprimals or portions.
9. True (p. 432)
10. True (p. 432)
11. True (p. 432)
12. False (p. 438)
13. True (p. 438)
14. False (p. 438)

CHAPTER 19

19A. Terminology

Answers will not be provided in answer key. All answers can be found in text.

19B. Multiple Choice

1. b
2. d
3. c
4. a
5. d
6. b

7. a
8. d
9. c
10. d
11. c
12. c

19C. Market Forms of Fish

1. drawn
2. pan-dressed
3. fillets

4. whole or round
5. steaks
6. butterflied fillets
7. wheel or center cut

19D. Short Answer

1. a. they cook evenly
   b. they cook quickly
2. a. translucent flesh becomes opaque
   b. flesh becomes firm
   c. flesh separates from the bones easily
   d. flesh begins to flake
3. a. shallow poach
   b. sauté
   c. broil
   d. bake
4. oily
   a. trout
   b. swordfish
   lean
   c. bass
   d. snapper

5. a. scallops
   b. lobster
   c. shrimp
   d. crab
6. a. baked stuffed shrimp
   b. oysters Rockefeller
   c. baked stuffed lobster
7. a. they are naturally tender
   b. they cook relatively quickly
8. a. eyes
   b. gills
   c. fins and scales
   d. smell

19E. Chapter Review

1. False (p. 471). Only fish processed under Type 1 inspection services are eligible for grading.
2. False (p. 470). Fish and shellfish inspections are voluntary and are performed in a fee-for-service program.
3. True (p. 457)
4. True (p. 485)
5. False (p. 469). Maine lobsters have meat both in their tails and claws and are considered superior in flavor to all other lobsters. Spiny lobsters primarily have meat in the tails.
6. False (p. 465). Atlantic hard-shell clams are also known as quahogs.
7. True (p. 464)
8. False (p. 491). En papillote is actually an example of steaming.
9. False (p. 470). In general, shellfish has less cholesterol than lamb and other meats.
10. True (p. 461)
11. True (p. 464)
12. False (p. 460). The only market form that monkfish is sold in is the tail (fillet).
13. False (p. 459). Surimi is very low in fat and relatively high in protein. Because of processing techniques, however, it has more sodium and fewer vitamins and minerals than the real fish or shellfish it replaces.
14. True (p. 457)
15. True (p. 463)

CHAPTER 20

20A. Terminology

Answers will not be provided in answer key. All answers can be found in text.

20B. Multiple Choice

1. d
2. b
3. b
4. d
5. b, c, d, f
6. c

20C. Identification

a. shell
b. yolk
c. white
d. chalaza

20D. Chapter Review

1. True (p. 536)
2. False (p. 536). Shell color has no effect on the quality (grade), flavor, or nutrition.
3. False (p. 544). When preparing French-style omelets the eggs are cooked without a filing, then tightly rolled onto a plate for service. The finished omelet can then be cut and filled as desired.
4. True (p. 538)
5. False (p. 539). The egg whites should be brought to room temperature to maximize the volume when whipping.
6. False (p. 537). Eggs should be store at temperatures below 40 degrees F. and at a relative humidity of 70-80%.
7. False (p. 538). Egg substitutes have a different flavor than real eggs and cannot be used in recipes where the eggs are required for thickening.
8. False (p. 539). Egg whites contain more than half of the protein and riboflavin, but no cholesterol.
9. False (p. 542). Egg whites coagulate at a lower temperature than yolks, so when preparing an egg white omelet, adjust your cooking time and temperature accordingly.
10. True (p. 537)

CHAPTER 21

21A. Terminology

Answers will not be provided in answer key. All answers can be found in text.

21B. Short Answer

1. a. Diced nutritional ingredient
   b. Thick batter
2. a. Pat food dry and dredge in flour (if desired).
   b. Dip item in batter and place directly in hot fat without the use of food baskets.
3. a. Product to be breaded
   b. Flour
   c. Egg wash
   d. Bread crumbs
   e. Pan to hold final product
4. Use one hand for dipping the food into the liquid ingredients and one hand to dip into the dry ingredients.

5.   Element   Effects

Element	Effects
a. Salt	fat becomes dark
b. Water	fat smokes
c. Overheating	fat foams
d. Food particles	fat develops flavors
e. Oxygen	fat becomes rancid

6. a. Helps to keep food moist
   b. Prevents excessive greasiness
7. a. The fat must be hot enough to quickly seal the surface of the food so it doesn't become excessively greasy.
   b. The fat shouldn't be so hot that the food's surface burns before the interior is cooked.
8. a. The color of the final product is an even, golden brown *providing that* the food is also cooked on the interior.
   b. Large items like fried chicken can be tested with a thermometer.
   c. The exterior of the fried product, including potatoes, should be crisp.
9. a. Flavor
   b. Smoke point
   c. Resistance to chemical breakdown
10. Fried foods
   a. should be kept under a heat lamp
   b. should be placed in a pan lined with absorbent paper on a rack.
   c. should not be stored in steam tables.

21C. Chapter Review

1. True (p. 570)
2. False (p. 563). This method is best used for foods that float, therefore the second basket is placed on top of the food to ensure total submersion in the hot fat.
3. False (p. 561). Fryolators are sized by the amount of fat they hold.
4. False (p. 568). It is preferred to cook and cool the main ingredient before mixing it with batter. Otherwise, since the frying time is relatively short in most instances, it is likely that the uncooked ingredient would not cook in time.
5. True (p. 562)
6. False (p. 563). Foods that are fried together should be the same size and thickness so they cook evenly.
7. True (p. 560)
8. True (p. 562)
9. True (p. 561)
10. False (p. 567). The primary purpose is leavening, flavor is an added benefit.
11. True (p. 561)
12. False (p. 562). Do not fill the basket while it is hanging over the fat as this allows unnecessary crumbs, salt, and food particles to fall into the fat, shortening its life.
13. True (p. 563)
14. True (p. 563)
15. False (p. 561). Deep-frying foods in a sauce pot on the stove top is discouraged because it is both difficult and dangerous. Recovery time is usually very slow, and temperatures are difficult to control. Also the fat can spill easily, leading to injuries or creating a fire hazard.
16. True (p. 561)

CHAPTER 22

22A. Terminology

Answers will not be provided in answer key. All answers can be found in text.

22B. Multiple Choice

1. b	6. c
2. c	7. c
3. b	8. d
4. c	9. b
5. a	10. b

22C. Matching

1. i	5. a	9. m	13. n
2. b	6. j	10. l	
3. f	7. g	11. c	
4. h	8. d	12. e	

22D. Chapter Review

1. True (p. 600)
2. False (p. 615). Pureed vegetables are usually prepared by baking, boiling, steaming, or microwaving.
3. False (p. 584). Green leafy vegetables and winter squash are generally not braised or stewed.
4. True (p. 599)
5. True (p. 577)
6. False (p. 600). Heat required in the canning process is what causes the contents of the can to lose nutrients and the texture to soften.
7. True (p. 589)
8. True (p. 598)
9. False (p. 587). They are usually stored at 40-60° F.
10. True (p. 601)
11. False (p. 601). Red and white vegetables such as red cabbage, beets, and cauliflower contain flavenoids.
12. False (p. 603). Testing the texture, looking for an al dente consistency, is generally the best determination of doneness.
13. False (p. 599). The ripening process of vegetables proceeds more rapidly in the presence of ethylene gas.
14. True (p. 602)
15. False (p. 599). The FDA classifies food irradiation as an additive.

CHAPTER 23

23A. Terminology

Answers will not be provided in answer key. All answers can be found in text.

23B. Short Answer

1. To allow the pasta ample space to move freely and so that the starches that are released don't cause the pasta to become gummy and sticky.
2. a. Wrapping the potato in foil causes it to steam instead of bake and the skin will be soggy.
   b. Microwaving also causes steaming to occur and causes the skin to be soggy.
3. a. Italian risotto
   b. Spanish paella
   c. Japanese sushi
4. This gives the dough a rich, yellow color, and the dough is more resilient to the machinery during high-scale production. It also produces pasta that has a lightly pitted surface, causing the pasta to absorb sauces well.
5. a. Duchesse + tomato concasse=Marquis
   b. Duchesse + chopped truffles, almond coating, and deep-fried=Berny
   c. Duchesse + pâte à choux=Dauphine
   d. Dauphine + grated parmesan, piped, and deep-fried=Lorette
6. a. Ribbon
   b. Tubes
   c. Shapes
7. a. Simmering
   b. Pilaf
   c. Risotto
8. a. The water softens the noodle strands.
   b. The bundles begin to separate.
   c. The noodles cook more evenly.

23C. Multiple Choice

1. a
2. c
3. d
4. d
5. c
6. b
7. b
8. b
9. b

23D. Chapter Review

1. True (p. 647)
2. True (p. 643)
3. True (p. 642)
4. False (p. 655). Semolina flour, although it makes the dough more yellow, makes a dough tougher and more difficult to work with.
5. True (p. 657)
6. False (p. 635). A yam is botanically different from both sweet and common potatoes. Although it is less sweet than a sweet potato, it can be used interchangeably.
7. False (p. 636). Potatoes should be stored between 50 and 60 degrees F.
8. False (p. 636). Waxy potatoes are best for these applications.
9. True (p. 654)
10. True (p. 658)
11. True (p. 640)
12. True (p. 647)

13. False (p. 645). The standard ratio for cooking rice is 2 parts liquid to 1 part rice.
14. True (p. 651)
15. False (p. 645). Generally cracked wheat and bulgur cannot be substituted for one another in recipes.
16. True (p. 646)

CHAPTER 24

24A. Terminology

Answers will not be provided in answer key. All answers can be found in text.

24B. Multiple Choice

1. b
2. b
3. c
4. c
5. d
6. a
7. c
8. d
9. b

24C. Short Answer

1. a. Cheese and other high-fat dairy products
   b. Most meats (especially if high in fat)
   c. Most emulsified dressings
2. a. The gas causes the greens to wilt.
   b. Accelerates spoilage
3. a. Buttermilk
   b. Vinegar
   c. Herbs
   d. Spices
   e. Vegetables
4. a. Bring mise en place up to room temperature.
   b. In the bowl of an electric mixer, whip the egg yolks until frothy.
   c. Add seasonings to the yolks and combine.
   d. Add a small amount of liquid from the recipe and combine.
   e. Begin whipping on high speed and slowly drizzle in oil until emulsion starts.
   f. After the emulsion forms, slow the mixer and add the oil a bit faster.
   g. When the mayonnaise is thick, add a small amount of the liquid from the recipe. Alternate this process with the oil until all incorporated.
   h. Taste, adjust seasonings, and refrigerate immediately.
5. a. liqueur
   b. fruit puree
   c. yogurt
   d. sweetener, such as honey

24D. Chapter Review

1. True (p. 691)
2. True (p. 684)
3. False (p. 687). Tender greens such as butterhead and baby lettuces benefit from hand-tearing, while hardy greens like Romain or Cos are acceptable to cut with a knife.

4. False (p. 695). Although tossed salads should in fact be dressed at the last possible moment, it is to prevent the greens from becoming soggy.
5. False (p. 686). Generally softer-leaved lettuces do tend to perish more quickly in storage than crisper-leaved varieties, however Iceberg is not a soft-leaved lettuce.
6. True (p. 695)
7. True (p. 688)
8. False (p. 690). The standard ratio of oil to vineger in a temporary emulsion is 3 parts to 1. The rest of the statement is true.
9. True (p. 689)
10. True (p. 693)

CHAPTER 25

25A. Terminology

Answers will not be provided in answer key. All answers can be found in text.

25B. Fill in the Blank

1. a. bananas   c. apples
   b. tomatoes   d. melons
2. A grayish cast or color on the fruit
3. *Vitamin C:*   citrus, melons, and strawberries
   Vitamin A: apricots, mangos, and kiwis
   Potassium: bananas, raisins, figs
4. Process the fruit into:
   a. sauces   c. jellies
   b. jams   d. preserves
5. a. irradiation   d. acidulation
   b. canning   e. drying
   c. freezing
6. a. apples   c. pears
   b. bananas   d. peaches
7. poaching
8. apples
9. gourd
10. grapes
11. batter
12. a. apples   d. bananas
    b. cherries   e. pineapples
    c. pears

25C. Product Identification

1. b   6. g
2. e   7. a
3. d   8. k
4. h   9. f
5. i   10. j

25D. Chapter Review

1. True (p. 743)
2. True (p. 742)
3. False (p. 742). Sulfur dioxide is added to prevent browning and extend the shelf life.
4. False (p. 741). Freezing is generally one of the worst preserving methods for preserving the natural appearance since all fruits are 75-95% water which seeps out of the fruit when it defrosts.
5. False (p. 739). The highest grade is U.S. Fancy.
6. True (p. 737)
7. True (p. 741)
8. False (p. 736). Papayas are also referred to as Paw Paws.
9. True (p. 734)
10. True (p. 737)
11. False (p. 730). Red Delicious apples are best for eating raw.
12. False (p. 732). Although stone fruits are commonly dried, or made into liqueurs and brandies, mangoes are not a stone fruit.
13. True (p. 738)
14. False (p. 735). Meat tenderizers contain enzymes similar to those found in pineapples and the seeds of kiwis and papayas.
15. True (p. 740)
16. True (p. 741)
17. False (p. 744). Fruits layed in a pan and sprinkled with a strudel topping and then baked are called crisps or crumbles.

CHAPTER 26

26A. Terminology

Answers will not be provided in answer key. All answers can be found in text.

26B. Short Answer

1. Hot, Cold
2. Protein
3. Human hands
4. Butter, mayonnaise, vegetable purees
5. Bound
6. Hot, open-faced
7. Reference: Page 768-769

26C. Multiple Choice

1. a
2. c
3. d
4. a

26D. Chapter Review

1. False (p. 763)
2. False (p. 764)
3. False (p. 765)
4. True (p. 768)
5. True (p. 768)
6. False (p. 769)

CHAPTER 27

27A. Terminology

Answers will not be provided in answer key. All answers can be found in text.

27B. Short Answer

1. a. basic forcemeat
   b. country-style forcemeat
   c. mousseline forcemeat
2. Add small quantities of crushed ice, bit by bit, to the machine while it is grinding.
3.

galantine	*ballottine*
a. uses whole chickens, ducks, etc.	uses poultry legs
b. all bones are removed	all bones are removed
c. cavity of bird is filled with forcemeat	cavity of leg is filled with forcemeat
d. it is wrapped in skin, plastic, cheesecloth	cooked without wrapping
e. it is poached	it is poached or braised
f. always served cold	usually served hot

4. a. keep a precise ratio of fat to other ingredients
   b. maintain temperatures below 40 degrees F. during preparation
   c. mix ingredients properly
5. a. to glaze, preventing drying out and oxidation of food
   b. to cut into decorative garnish
   c. to add flavor and shine
   d. to bind mousses and salads
   e. to fill cooked pâtés én croûte

27C. Multiple Choice

1. a	4. a
2. c	5. d
3. c	6. b

27D. Matching

1. f	3. e
2. i	4. d

5. b 8. c
6. a 9. j
7. g

27E. Chapter Review

1. False (p. 789). Mousseline forcemeats can only be made out of meats, poultry, fish, or shellfish.
2. False (p. 802). The best type of mold to use is a collapsible, hinged, thin metal pan.
3. True (p. 805)
4. False (p. 789). Eggs and egg whites are used as a primary binding agent in some styles of forcemeats.
5. True (p. 808)
6. False (p. 789). When marinating forcemeat ingredients before grinding, the trend today is to marinate them for shorter periods to let the natural flavors of the ingredients dominate.
7. True (p. 809)
8. True (p. 798)
9. False (p. 804). A fresh ham is made from the pig's hind leg.
10. False (p. 790). After testing a forcemeat's texture and finding it too firm, a little cream should be added to fix the problem.
11. True (p. 795)
12. True
13. False (p. 801). Chopped chicken liver should be eaten within a day or two of its preparation whereas rillettes will keep for several weeks under refrigeration.
14. True (p. 808)
15. True (p. 810)

CHAPTER 28

28A. Terminology

Answers will not be provided in answer key. All answers can be found in text.

28B. Multiple Choice

1. d
2. b
3. c
4. b

28C. Fill in The Blanks

1. a. Fish
   b. Rice
   c. Seasonings
2. Brochettes

3. Pan-fried or deep-fried
4. Three, four to five
5. One

28D. Short Answer

1. Reference: Page 962
2. Reference: Page 964
3. Reference: Page 967
4. Reference: Page 975
5. Reference: Page 831
6. Reference: Page 835

28E. Matching

1. E
2. B
3. A

28F. Chapter Review

1. False (p. 830). Appetizers are usually the first course before the evening meal.
2. True (p. 835)
3. True (p. 835)
4. False (p. 835)
5. False (p. 831)
6. False (p. 831)
7. True (p. 835)
8. False (p. 835)
9. False (p. 837)

CHAPTER 29

29A. Terminology

Answers will not be provided in answer key. All answers can be found in text.

29B. Matching

1. d	6. e
2. i	7. a
3. f	8. j
4. b	9. g
5. c	

29C. Multiple Choice

1. d	3. c	5. d
2. b	4. b	6. a

7. d   10. a   13. a
8. d   11. d
9. c   12. b

29D. Chapter Review

1. False (p. 866). Self-rising flour is all-purpose flour with salt and baking powder added to it.
2. False (p. 865). Glutenin and gliadin are the proteins which, when introduced to moisture and manipulated, form gluten.
3. True (p. 877)
4. False (p. 878). Unsweetened chocolate is 100% chocolate liquor.
5. True (p. 879)
6. True (p. 878)
7. True (p. 865)
8. False (p. 865). Flour derived from this portion of the endosperm is finer than other flours.
9. True (p. 866)
10. False (p. 867). Unopened flour should be stored in the manner described, except it is also very important to store it away from strong odors, as it will absorb them easily.
11. True (p. 867)
12. True (p. 874). In addition to these qualities, unsalted butter tends to be preferred because it is generally fresher than salted butter.
13. True (p. 883)
14. True (p. 881)
15. False (p. 873). Most bakeshop ingredients combine completely with liquids, but fats do not.
16. False (p. 873). Oils may not be substituted for solid shortenings in recipes.
17. True (p. 875)
18. False (p. 876). The white coating is actually vanillin and the bean can still be used.
19. True (p. 878)
20. False (p. 878). The refining process for chocolate varies from country to country. For example, Swiss and German chocolate is the smoothest, followed by English chocolates. American chocolate has a noticeably more grainy texture.

CHAPTER 30

30A. Terminology

Answers will not be provided in answer key. All answers can be found in text.

30B. Short Answer

1. The bitter or soapy flavor, and sometimes yellow coloring, is often caused by too much baking soda that may not have been properly mixed into the batter.

2. Baking soda can only release carbon dioxide to the extent that there is also an acid present in the formula. If the soda/acid reaction alone is insufficient to leaven the product, baking powder is needed for additional leavening.

3. Batters/doughs that may sit for some time before baking often use double-acting baking powder, which has a second leavening action that is activated only with the application of heat.

4. The higher fat content in the creaming method shortens the strands of gluten and therefore makes the final product more tender.

5. Softening the fat makes it easier to cream it with the sugar and therefore creates better aeration.

6. Overmixing the batter.

7. A scone is seen by many as a rich biscuit that also has butter and eggs in it. It is speculated that biscuits, at least the American form of the word, contain a less expensive type of fat, such as lard, and will omit the eggs.

30C. Chapter Review

1. False (p. 891). All purpose flour is used in all of these methods.
2. True (p. 893)
3. True (p. 888)
4. False (p. 888). Baking powder already contains both an acid and a base and therefore only moisture is needed to induce the release of gases.
5. False (p. 888). All quick breads use chemical leavening agents and because they don't need to ferment, like yeast-leavened doughs, they are considered "quick".
6. True (p. 890)
7. False (p. 892). Fats used in the muffin method should be in the liquid form.
8. False (p. 896). The leavening agent was there, so the assumption should be that the oven temperature was too low.
9. True (p. 888)
10. False (p. 889). Batters and doughs made with single-acting baking powder should be baked as soon as they are assembled and mixed together.
11. False (p. 888). Baking soda releases carbon dioxide gas if both an acid and moisture are present; heat is not necessary for leavening to occur.
12. False (p. 889). Shortcakes are made using the biscuit method.
13. True (p. 895)
14. False (p. 895). Once a waffle iron is seasoned it should not be washed.

CHAPTER 31

31A. Terminology

Answers will not be provided in answer key. All answers can be found in text.

31B. Multiple Choice

1. c		6. a
2. d		7. d
3. c		8. a
4. b		9. c
5. b		10. a

31C. Short Answer

1. a. The yeast, liquid, and approximately one half of the flour are combined to make a thick batter known as a sponge, which is allowed to rise until bubbly and doubled in size.
   b. Then the salt, fat, sugar, and remaining flour are added. The dough is then kneaded and allowed to rise again. This creates a different flavor and a lighter texture than breads made with the straight dough method.
2. The organism is considered dormant because virtually all of the moisture has been removed, which helps to increase the shelf life, among other things.
3. a. product size
   b. the thermostat's accuracy
   c. crust color
   d. tapping loaf on the bottom and listening for hollow sound
4. a. croissants
   b. Danish pastries
   c. non-yeast-leavened pastry
5. Halve the specified weight of compressed yeast when substituting dry yeast in a formula.
6. Combine all ingredients and mix.
7. a. Scale ingredients
   b. Mix and knead dough
   c. Ferment dough
   d. Punch down dough
   e. Portion dough
   f. Round portions
   g. Shape portions
   h. Proof products
   i. Bake products
   j. Cool and store finished products

31D. Chapter Review

1. True (p. 913). More specifically, though, it occurs just after fermentation.
2. False (p. 908). Salt's primary role in bread making is conditioning gluten, making it stronger and more elastic.
3. True (p. 912)
4. True (p. 917)
5. False (p. 916). Underproofing results in poor volume and texture.
6. True (p. 920)
7. True (p. 909)
8. False (p. 909). Active dry yeast contains virtually no moisture.
9. True (p. 909)
10. False (p. 910). Prior to commercial yeast production bakers relied on starters to leaven their breads. Today starters are generally used to provide consistency and reliability.
11. True (p. 909)
12. False (p. 912). Overkneading is rarely a problem.

CHAPTER 32

32A. Terminology

Answers will not be provided in answer key. All answers can be found in text.

32B. Short Answer

1. a. chiffon   b. cooked juice   c. cream
2. a. cream   b. chiffon   b. cooked juice   d. cheesecake
3. a. baked fruit   b. custard
4. a. lattice coverings
   b. pie top crusts
   c. prebaked shells later to be filled with cooked fillings
5. It is a rich, non-flaky, and sturdier dough than flaky or mealy dough due to the addition of egg yolks and the blending of the fat.
6. When the crust has a potential of becoming soggy, as in the making of custard and cooked fruit pies.
7. One can have better control because you can feel the fat being incorporated and therefore prevent overmixing.
8. It is cooked before baking.
9. The ratio of sugar to egg whites.
10. a. vol au vents   c. feuilletées
    b. Napoleons   d. bouchées

32C. Multiple Choice

1. d
2. b
3. b
4. c
5. d

32D. Chapter Review

1. True (p. 964)
2. False (p. 952). Strawberries, pineapples, and blueberries would be more appropriate.
3. True (p. 949)
4. True (p. 954)
5. False (p. 959). A typical ratio for crumb crusts consists of one part melted butter to two parts sugar to four parts crumbs.
6. True (p. 943)
7. False (p. 944). Pâte sucrée should be used specifically over flaky and mealy doughs because it is less flaky and due to the addition of the egg yolks, is still tender, but is stronger to withstand the removal of the tart pan during service.
8. True (p. 964)
9. False (p. 952). A cooked juice filling should be combined with a prebaked or crumb crust.
10. False (p. 956). Baked fruit pies may be stored at room temperature until service.
11. True (p. 943)
12. False (p. 943). An American gâteau refers to any cake-type dessert.

CHAPTER 33

33A. Terminology

Answers will not be provided in answer key. All answers can be found in text.

33B. Basic Cake Mixes Revised

Reference: Pages 998–1005

33C. Matching I - Ingredient Functions

1. f
2. a
3. e
4. c
5. d
6. g

33D. Matching II - Frostings

1. d
2. f
3. b
4. e
5. a
6. g

33E. Cake Mixing Categories

1. b
2. b
3. a
4. b
5. a

6. a
7. a
8. b
9. a
10. a

33F. Frostings Revised

Reference: Pages 1010–1019

33G. Fill in the Blank

1. decreased
   underwhipped
   increased
   25 degrees
2. a. Appearance
   b. Touch
   c. Taste tester should come out clean

3. 325° F
   375° F
4. decorators icing
5. flour
   shortening
   oil

33H. Chapter Review

1. False (p. 1010). All cakes should be left away from drafts which may cause them to collapse. Cakes should not be refrigerated as rapid cooling will cause cracking.
2. True (p. 1025)
3. True (p. 1008)
4. True (p. 1007)
5. False (p. 1003)
6. True (p. 1006)
7. False (p. 1006). The results from package mixes are consistent and acceptable to most customers.
8. False (p. 1000). High-ratio cakes require emulsified shortenings to absorb the large amounts of sugar and liquid in the formula.

CHAPTER 34

34A. Terminology

Answers will not be provided in answer key. All answers can be found in text.

34B. Short Answer

1. Reference: Page 1040
2. Reference: Page 1041
3. Reference: Page 1054
4. Reference: Page 1046
5. Reference: Page 1043
6. Reference: Page 1051
7. Reference: Page 1058

34C. Fill in the Blank

1. zabaglione
2. mousseline
   Italian merangue
3. Bavarians
   chiffons
   mousses
   crèmes Chantilly
4. a. egg whites will whip to a better volume
   b. the two mixtures are more easily incorporated

34D. Chapter Review

1. False (p. 1041)
2. True (p. 1046). A frozen soufflé is a creamy custard mixture thickened with gelatin, lightened with whipped egg whites or whipped cream, and placed in a soufflé dish wrapped with a tall paper collar.
3. False (p. 1055). A sherbet contains milk and/or egg yolks for creaminess.
4. True (p. 1055)
5. True (p. 1056)
6. True (p. 1044)

CHAPTER 35

35A. Terminology

Answers will not be provided in answer key. All answers can be found in text.

35B. Fill in the Blank

1. Hippen masse
2. Texture, shape, color
3. Cutting, molding
4. Size
5. Focal point
6. a. Flavor   d. Color
   b. Moisture   e. Texture
   c. Flow
7. Cold
8. a. Height
   b. Texture
9. a. To show the chef's attention to detail
   b. To provide visual appeal
   c. To ensure even cooking of the product

35C. Chapter Review

1. True (p. 1086)
2. False (p. 1090). The food should always be the focal point of any plate.
3. True (p. 1089)
4. False (p. 1090). Dusting of a plate should be done before the food is plated.
5. False (p. 1093). A squeeze bottle would be a good choice of equipment for preparing sauce drawings.
6. False (p. 1093). An equally important concept is that the sauces need to be thick enough to hold a pattern and all sauces used in the drawing need to be the same viscosity.
7. True (p. 1085)
8. False (p. 1090). Plate dusting is most commonly associated with pastry presentations.

CHAPTER 36

36A. Terminology

Answers will not be provided in answer key. All answers can be found in text.

36B. Short Answer

1. a. Offer dishes featuring different principal ingredients
   b. Offer foods cooked by different cooking methods
   c. Offer foods with different colors
   d. Offer foods with different textures
2. Reference p. 1101-1102
3. a. Use a double-sided buffet
   b. Use a single-sided buffet, divided into tow, three or more zones, each of which offers the identical foods.
   c. Divide the menu among various stations, scattered throughout the room, each station devoted to a different type of food.
4. a. Choose foods that hold well
   b. Cook small amounts of delicate foods
   c. Ladle a small amount of sauce in the bottom of the pan before adding sliced meats
   d. Keep chafing dish closed whenever possible

36C. Multiple Choice

1. c
2. b
3. d
4. c

36D. Chapter Review

1. True (p. 1098)
2. False (p. 1098)
3. False (p. 1100)
4. True (p. 1100)
5. True (p. 1104)
6. False (p. 1105)
7. False (p. 1106)
8. True (p. 1111)
9. False (p. 1111)
10. True (p. 1112)